"Beware. This is not a youth min␣␣ is not about keeping our kids, bu␣␣ covering a new secret for growing your youth group, but recovering an old truth about transforming your community of faith. With a love for young people borne out of years of ministry and a penetrating theological gaze honed in years of scholarship, Sharon Galgay Ketcham challenges church leaders to grasp the moment and the opportunity that is upon us as we experience droves of young people leaving the church behind. Their longing for reciprocal relationships forces us to reconsider everything we assume that the church is supposed to do. *Reciprocal Church* will require you to rethink everything you think you know about youth ministry and everything you forgot about being the church."

Tod Bolsinger, vice president and chief of leadership formation at Fuller Seminary, author of *Canoeing the Mountains: Christian Leadership in Uncharted Territory*

"Sharon Galgay Ketcham is the most important youth ministry voice you've yet to hear of; with *Reciprocal Church* this will be rectified! You hold an exciting book in your hand (or beaming from your e-reader). It's an engaging read with important thoughts on nearly every page. Take time with it. If you do, you'll find your imagination ignited and Sharon Ketcham will become a new dialogue partner in your ministry."

Andrew Root, professor of youth and family ministry at Luther Seminary (USA), author of *Exploding Stars, Dead Dinosaurs, and Zombies: Youth Ministry in the Age of Science*

"*Reciprocal Church* establishes Sharon Galgay Ketcham as a leading voice in the field of youth ministry. This book offers youth ministers (and professors of youth ministry) a theologically significant—and refreshingly sane—voice to guide them in their daily ministries."

Kenda Creasy Dean, Mary D. Synnott Professor of Youth, Church, and Culture, Princeton Theological Seminary, author of *Almost Christian*

"Providing real space and place for the young has only recently become the most important conversation in youth ministry, but finally we're taking notice. Research has consistently shown that young people feel an overwhelming sense of disconnection, isolation, and abandonment, even in the church. As we attempt to engage and support emerging generations, we need help. As a researcher, Dr. Ketcham guides me deeper into the why and what of helping the young to flourish. As a pastor, Sharon reminds me that our kids are a viable and vital part of us as she teaches me that we need them as much as they need us. This is an important book for all of us as we work to break down our walls and invite young people to the table alongside of us."

Chap Clark, author of *Hurt 2.0* and *Adoptive Church,* pastor at St. Andrew's Presbyterian Church, Newport Beach, CA

"In a time when reports persist about young people leaving the institutional church, *Reciprocal Church* is a dynamic, passionately written text that offers fresh insight about ecclesiology, youth ministry, and the importance of Christian practices. Ketcham challenges people of faith to question and reframe their assumptions about the nature and function of the church. *Reciprocal Church* is not a feel-good book; rather, this book is convicting. At every turn, Ketcham calls the church to actually *be* the church. Reading this book leaves me feeling challenged, convicted, refreshed, and hopeful all at the same time!"

Sarah F. Farmer, associate research scholar, Yale Center for Faith & Culture, Adolescent Faith and Flourishing Program

"The reality is undeniable: far too many students leave our youth ministries and enter the post–high school years hitting the pause or stop button on their faith. Sharon Galgay Ketcham offers a path beyond the youth ministry status quo that we must consider. If our churches and youth ministries are to work with parents to nurture children and teens, then we must re-evaluate what we've been doing and make adjustments that result in judging the effectiveness of our congregational efforts to ensure the future flourishing of our students."

Walt Mueller, founder and president of the Center for Parent/Youth Understanding

"*Reciprocal Church* is not just a book about youth ministry but lays the foundation for a conversation that could be impactful among all levels of church leadership. Sharon Galgay Ketcham deconstructs some prevailing current perspectives affecting youth ministry and then challenges her readers to reconstruct their vision for a church that is robust, theologically driven, and intentional in connecting youth with the entire community of faith. By clarifying values and practices that encourage a *reciprocal*, relational connection between youth and the rest of the church, the author helps us take a significant step in sharpening our awareness of how to address the spiritual drift we see among youth and young adults."

Jana Sundene, associate professor of Christian ministries at Trinity International University, coauthor of *Shaping the Journey of Emerging Adults*

"You are about to sit down with a book from a master teacher who cares deeply about young people and the church. Dr. Sharon Galgay Ketcham has been a longtime leader in the conversations regarding the faith development and church participation of young people. Her research has drawn out some helpful language and guiding principles that can serve church leaders well. This book is a source of hope and offers a thoughtful and practical way forward, giving churches the foundation and the means to see vibrant renewal in the lives of their young people."

Terry Linhart, editor of *Teaching the Next Generations*, professor of Christian ministries at Bethel College

"Sharon Galgay Ketcham has given us a fresh way of thinking about youth ministry, teenagers, and the local church. It's delightfully creative, theologically thoughtful, and written with a clarity and hopefulness that invites further conversation and practical steps forward. This is what you get when you read a book written by a serious scholar who's also a passionate youth worker, a seasoned teacher and mentor, an experienced mom, and a lover of Christ and his church."

Duffy Robbins, professor of youth ministry, Grove City College

"In *Reciprocal Church*, youth workers, local church, and denominational leaders, together with concerned parents, will find astute theological, sociological, and practical reflection to aid them in the task of engaging young people today with the future in mind. I wholeheartedly concur with the disruptive innovation that Sharon encourages where decades-old approaches to student ministry are concerned. Indeed, young people today do not present a problem for the church to solve; rather, they represent and can become the answer to problems the church will face long-term."

Mark DeYmaz, founding pastor of Mosaic Church of Central Arkansas, president of Mosaix Global Network

"Sharon Galgay Ketcham has written a book for anyone who loves the faith life of young people and the work of youth ministry. But she lays down the ultimate challenge as she asks all of us in youth ministry to make *church* a serious player in that enterprise. Filled with engaging metaphors and provocative examples, this book will help you and your ministry teams think and see and recreate your youth ministry."

Nancy S. Going, executive director, Vibrant Faith Ministries

"Sharon Galgay Ketcham is a brilliant, winsome, and attentive teacher. Her observational skills rival those of many standup comics, and she can trade youth ministry war stories with anyone. But it's her richly informed theological thinking about current church practices and their impact on young people that had me appreciatively slow clapping one minute and clenching my jaw in conviction the next. God is stirring among his people, calling us to live like the reconciled people we claim to be. *Reciprocal Church* is the latest evidence of this hopeful movement, and I pray it will especially benefit the youth ministry wing of the church."

Dave Rahn, senior ministry advisor, Youth for Christ USA

RECIPROCAL
CHURCH

**BECOMING A
COMMUNITY
WHERE FAITH
FLOURISHES
BEYOND
HIGH SCHOOL**

SHARON GALGAY KETCHAM

IVP Books

An imprint of InterVarsity Press
Downers Grove, Illinois

InterVarsity Press
P.O. Box 1400, Downers Grove, IL 60515-1426
ivpress.com
email@ivpress.com

InterVarsity Press® is the book-publishing division of InterVarsity Christian Fellowship/USA®, a movement of students and faculty active on campus at hundreds of universities, colleges, and schools of nursing in the United States of America, and a member movement of the International Fellowship of Evangelical Students. For information about local and regional activities, visit intervarsity.org.

All Scripture quotations, unless otherwise indicated, are taken from The Holy Bible, New International Version®, NIV®. Copyright © 1973, 1978, 1984, 2011 by Biblica, Inc.™ Used by permission of Zondervan. All rights reserved worldwide. www.zondervan.com. The "NIV" and "New International Version" are trademarks registered in the United States Patent and Trademark Office by Biblica, Inc.™

While any stories in this book are true, some names and identifying information may have been changed to protect the privacy of individuals.

Cover design and image composite: David Fassett
Interior design: Jeanna Wiggins
Images: watercolor blue waves: © Nebula Cordata / iStock / Getty Images Plus
    marble texture: © NK08gerd / iStock / Getty Images Plus
    pastel background: © andipantz / DigitalVision Vectors / Getty Images
    abstract layer background: © wacomka / iStock / Getty Images Plus
    brushed gold background: © Studiocasper / E+ / Getty Images
    old tree: © The photography Factory / Getty Images

ISBN 978-0-8308-4148-6 (print)
ISBN 978-0-8308-7388-3 (digital)

Printed in the United States of America ∞

InterVarsity Press is committed to ecological stewardship and to the conservation of natural resources in all our operations. This book was printed using sustainably sourced paper.

Library of Congress Cataloging-in-Publication Data

Names: Ketcham, Sharon Galgay, 1971- author.
Title: Reciprocal church : becoming a community where faith flourishes beyond
  high school / Sharon Galgay Ketcham.
Description: Downers Grove : InterVarsity Press, 2018. | Includes
  bibliographical references.
Identifiers: LCCN 2018028337 (print) | LCCN 2018033169 (ebook) | ISBN
  9780830873883 (eBook) | ISBN 9780830841486 (pbk. : alk. paper)
Subjects: LCSH: Church. | Intergenerational relations—Religious
  aspects—Christianity.
Classification: LCC BV640 (ebook) | LCC BV640 .K48 2018 (print) | DDC
  253—dc23
LC record available at https://lccn.loc.gov/2018028337

P   25   24   23   22   21   20   19   18   17   16   15   14   13   12   11   10   9   8   7   6   5   4   3   2   1

Y   37   36   35   34   33   32   31   30   29   28   27   26   25   24   23   22   21   20   19   18

IN HONOR OF MY MOM

(1942–2012)

You always knew before I did

CONTENTS

RECIPROCAL CHURCH

W E SHARE A COMMON INTEREST. We want young people—our kids and all kids—to flourish. We long for them to dig deep roots into the Christian faith. I think it is safe to assume this impulse prompted you to pick up this book. You can also assume this reason drove me to write it.

What is the reciprocal church? The word *reciprocal* provides us with multiple images. You might think of a reciprocal trade agreement between two or more countries. These intend to increase trade flow for mutual, economic benefit. The design of a mechanical device such as a reciprocal engine takes advantage of opposing motions such as up and down or back and forth. Reciprocation involves a type of motion. Unlike linear motion that follows a straight line or rotary motion that moves in a circle, a reciprocal church's motion is a push and pull or back and forth between persons. Much like a number (3) multiplied by its reciprocal (1/3) equals one, the reciprocal church benefits from the body of Christ's multiplying effect, which also makes us *one*. Take a peek at this book's cover art. Notice the reciprocal motion amid the layers of color intersecting with steeples and young faces. A reciprocal church trusts that the push and pull motion among people is to our advantage as the Spirit's multiplying effect makes us Christ's church. An inspiring vision, and a challenging path.

THE RENEWAL PLAN

I am thirteen and sitting in a church parking lot with my mom. My heels dig in as do hers. I am kid number three, so Mom is pretty adept at knowing when to push and when to release control. So when she pushes hard, I know my resistance is futile. My family is in the middle of a tumultuous time following our move from Texas to Germany. My brother starts a new school as a senior in high school, my sister remains in college in Texas, my dad faces tremendous responsibility in his new position, and my mom gets up every day to help each of us gain our footing. We must adapt to a new culture, a new language, new road signs, and new friends. Needless to say, the challenges my family face are taking a toll. And me? I have a freshly molded piece of plastic strapped around my body that I get to wear 24/7 to prevent my scoliosis from progressing. This final blow crushes what remains of my childhood confidence.

We are sitting in front of this church because my mom is forcing me to go inside and join a youth choir. She knows what I need before I know what questions to ask. And she is right. I encounter Jesus with this community and confirm the faith my parents taught me.

My faith experience sets the stage for a lifelong conviction: God gifts and empowers young people to renew the church. After graduating from college with a ministry degree, I spend a decade serving in the local church until I come to the end of what I know. Certainly, I can attest to God's transforming movement in the lives of young people during these years, but something is not quite right. I see the early signs long before news headlines sound the alarm that rising generations are leaving the church in unprecedented numbers. Amid what many would call a successful youth ministry, faith roots do not appear deep enough. How then could it be true that God wants young people to renew the church?

These experiences inaugurate my search for an answer to the reality that continues to unfold before us. The following pages capture years of researching, listening, experimenting, and clarifying. One thing is abundantly clear. My earlier vision of God using young people to renew the church took an unexpected turn. I envisioned young people as the heroes of this story whose passion would break in and spur us, the church, toward renewal. I did not anticipate that young people would be lead characters in a dramatic tragedy. Losing young people from our churches is what is finally capturing our attention.

The following pages will cast a vision for your community to become a reciprocal church and act as a catalyst for conversations and decisions in your churches and ministries. For each chapter, you will find a set of questions to assist you and leaders in your churches or ministries as you reflect on your particular circumstances. Part one of the book casts a theological vision for the reciprocal church, and part two defines values and practices inherent to becoming a community where faith might flourish. In chapter one we will explore the troubling loss of young people from our churches, evaluate the strengths and limitations of available solutions, and clarify specific aspects of culture in which we are all swimming. In chapter two, I pose three answers to a pressing theological question: how have we understood the relationship between young people and the church? We will explore how young people might end up believing this relationship is superfluous, the ways churches often treat the relationship as supportive, and why this relationship is actually vital.

> I did not anticipate that young people would be lead characters in a dramatic tragedy. Losing young people from our churches is what is finally capturing our attention.

The work of theology often involves examining our present conceptions of the Christian faith and evaluating whether these remain faithful to the biblical witness and our historic creeds and confessions.

By retrieving lost understanding or revising past conceptions, we do this work to express the faith in ways that make sense to us today and speak authentically to both the past and our present experiences. When you turn to chapters three to five, expect to join me in this work. I invite you to reflect theologically on your churches and ministries as you read the ways I describe the vital relationship shared among Christians. These chapters are progressive and build on one another. I offer a theological vision: we share a vital identity as God's people (chap. 3); Christ's present reconciling activity determines the vital purpose for our relationships (chap. 4); and relationships are an avenue for the Spirit to transform you, me, and us (chap. 5).

RECIPROCAL VALUES AND PRACTICES

We need to spend a little bit longer exploring how I use the terms *values* and *practices* in chapters six to ten. Values involve a reciprocating motion between and among people, and include: memory (chap. 6), mutuality (chap. 7), contribution (chaps. 8-9), and maturity (chap. 10). These values are the launching point for practices. Thanks to the powerful writings of people like Dorothy Bass, Adele Calhoun, James K. A. Smith, and Mike King, we are working to incorporate old and new practices into churches and youth ministries.[1] Practices focus on *what we do* and often stand in contrast to a more common approach that emphasizes *what we know*. Before I focus on practices, I will first take time to unfold the values that drive them. I define values as sustaining ideals shared by members of a community.

Since values are not always evident, I quickly deduce the annual ski trip is a problem. The entire youth ministry revolves around a three-generation tradition of packing teenagers into a chartered bus at 10 p.m. on December 25 (oh yes, Christmas night) and traversing the United States in search of Colorado powder. Group pictures line the walls of the youth room, and stories from past trips have a minimum ten-year life expectancy. Attendance at youth events climbs before the trip as evangelistic efforts double. The bulk of the youth ministry budget goes toward the expedition, and all ski-trip veterans believe this trip can almost guarantee a teenager's commitment to Christ. But then we return home. The literal mountaintop experience ends, and attendance drops radically in the weeks following. A small number of young people continue to meet regularly for the remainder of the year, anticipating next year's trip.

After a trip or two, I decide to change this long-standing tradition. You can imagine the scene: testimonies pouring in about lives that were transformed, endless expressions of unfiltered anger, and even a homemade video by kids begging for me to reconsider. Leaders, parents, and kids unite to save the ski trip.

Alas, my inexperience is evident because I miss what is driving this tradition. I only see the skis, the cost, and the singular focus. A closer look reveals something beautiful just below the surface. A twenty-four-hour bus ride full of authentic conversations. Long ski-lift journeys up 4,500-foot mountains, where young people marvel at God's creation and their place in it. Concentrated time away to confess sins, profess faith, seek healing, discover dreams, and live in community. Why is the trip the centerpiece of this youth ministry? I realize that this trip is where they encounter God and one another—a deeply shared *value*. When I push back on the trip, I stomp on sacred ground.

Values are sustaining ideals shared by members of a community. They undergird and shape ideas, priorities, attitudes, and behaviors. Although individuals certainly hold values, the specific values outlined in the following chapters focus on the reciprocal motion necessary to become a Christian community. These values include four attributes.

SUSTAINING VALUES

First, values in a reciprocal church are *shared ideals* we strive to reach. They mark what is ahead of us and, like a compass, provide a point of orientation. The cynic is prone to mock the idealist in the crowd for being naive and impractical. Yet where would we be without the idealist who relentlessly hopes against the odds? We strive toward our ideals. Ideals must also be sustaining. Like a runner's vision of crossing the marathon finish line, ideals inspire us when we climb steep hills. Communities need nourishing ideals that stimulate hope and persistence amid challenges. In a sense, ideals need to be unattainable (maybe even slightly unrealistic) to be worthy of our allegiance. They are bigger than us. Yet we will tire of our ideals if we cannot make progress toward them. Sustaining ideals best encourage persistence when we can see we have made progress along the way.

Second, holding values is an *act of faith* because they gain our confidence, and we trust them to be both true and beneficial. The community believes the value is important, maybe even essential. Most Americans feel this way about freedom. We trust that freedom will benefit our democratic society. Because of this, we willingly support efforts to maintain and even defend our freedom. Similarly, values of a reciprocal church are what communities order their common life around, use to set priorities, and, yes, even defend, because we believe they are worthy. Maintaining these values over time will require courage. In a 2002 *Harvard Business Review* article, Patrick Lencioni warns, "If you're not willing to accept the pain real values incur, don't bother going to the trouble of formulating a values statement."[2] Why pain? Because shared values set limits on our freedom and behaviors. We will only make such sacrifices because we have faith and confidence that what we value is trustworthy.

This leads to the third attribute. Values are *expressible*, meaning the community can describe and recognize them. Even though values can be difficult to capture in words, expressing them is crucial for a community to share a value. Moreover, words function in the social realm. Words shape our experiences just as our experiences give meaning to our words. These reciprocal church values can seep through the fabric of our communities with a common language understood best by those involved because they recognize the meaning behind the words. People can also model the values in ways that instruct and provide nuance that words are unable to capture.

Sometimes the value is explicit. The other day my son bounds into the house, grabs the remote from his younger sister, and abruptly changes the station. Typically, a sibling argument would break out, but my daughter knows what is going on and finds satisfaction in an eye roll. His NFL team is playing the last two minutes of a close game. Our family knows the explicit value driving the sudden disruption. Yet more frequently we express values implicitly, and these require decoding by outsiders. The ski trip scenario is a case in point. Those involved in that youth ministry implicitly know the shared value even without articulating it. I am the outsider, and it takes a while (and a good bit of turmoil) for me to decipher it.

We also express values in our dispositions or attitudes. What draws and repels you, what you ponder and dream, what you care for deeply, and what you fear all express values. The same is true of our habits and behaviors. We express what we value with our time, money, and choices. Values cannot be reduced to what people do, yet they undergird what we do. In this way, values are always accompanied by practices in the community since they shape who we are as well as what we do.

Last, the reciprocal church values I propose here are intended to be *malleable.* They are more like pieces of clay than concrete. Once dry, concrete is rigid and unable to adapt to new environments. Clay, however, offers the material for creative forms. It can be stretched, molded, or fashioned while remaining the same lump of clay. Like clay, these values are neither firm boundaries nor limiting forces. Yet also like clay they provide the substance awaiting creative interpretation by real people in real places with real experiences. A community that finds meaning in these values will have to shape them to fit its particular identity. It should be expected that communities work out these values as new voices join, as the environment changes, as distinct questions arise. The values should emerge in a particular form. It may be that some contexts require a piece of the clay to be cut off or an additional lump to be added for the community to adopt the value.

Why? *Because values only have meaning as people adopt them and creatively give them shape.* This also means that these values need to be made of substantive material that can withstand interpretation and reinterpretation by communities over time.

The reciprocal values, which are outlined in chapters six to ten, intend to be sustaining ideals shared by members of a community. They should inspire our persistence amid adversity as well as provide encouragement when we make progress toward them. I hope these values gain your confidence as you determine whether they are trustworthy and true. I will first define each value and give you an aerial view so that practices can organically emerge in your church and ministry.

VALUES PRODUCE PRACTICES

I confess I am directionally challenged. This is a gracious way of saying I have *no* sense of direction. The invention of the GPS system is a lifeline for someone like me. My brother-in-law comes to Boston for a conference, and I happily drive into the city to take him to dinner. Unlike planned cities such as DC or Dallas, Boston has organically emerged into a lovely jumble of twists and turns. Ah, but I have GPS. I punch in the address and fearlessly start driving. Unfortunately, my GPS is one of the early models that struggles to maintain a signal in cities. It does not take long for the tall buildings to block the signal and for the infamous "recalculating" voice to echo over and over as I drive in circles around the same areas. Because I lack an aerial view of the city, I am at the mercy of the step-by-step instructions.

We can make the same mistakes in ministry. It is much easier to open a box, locate the instructions, and put a ministry together like IKEA furniture. But you already know that does not work, or you would not have picked up this book. Those days are long gone in youth ministry. Learning these values and discerning what form and shape they might take in your particular context will take time and effort. That said, each chapter will also include suggested practices and some concrete ideas. These practices flow directly from the value, but they should not be mistaken for step-by-step instructions.

Although our concern for young people frames this book and many examples fill these pages, I hope you see by now that the reciprocal church is a theological shift for churches and ministries who find themselves wondering where to go from here. You will quickly discover that my proposal doesn't matter if young people are the only age group under consideration. I begin deep in the youth ministry trenches, but by the time we reach the end, our local churches are on center stage. The loss of rising generations from our churches means we need to reflect on the church—and resist treating young people as a problem to solve. Thank you for joining me in this theological journey, and I pray the reciprocal motion between these pages, your reflection, and the Spirit's wisdom will result in persons and communities being raised in Christ (Colossians 3:1) to be a people for God's reign (1 Peter 2:9), a temple learning to be a dwelling place for the Spirit (Ephesians 2:22), and a body carrying out the ministries of Christ (Ephesians 4:16).

I still believe young people will be a source of renewal in Christ's church, and pray for the Spirit to enable a reciprocating motion among us.

> **The reciprocal church is a theological shift for US churches that find themselves wondering where to go from here.**

PART 1

A THEOLOGICAL VISION FOR THE RECIPROCAL CHURCH

EATING MELON ON TUESDAYS

YOUNG PEOPLE AND FAITH

THE FAMILIAR REPORTS ARE LOUD AND CLEAR. We hear the news on Facebook, in our Twitter feed, and through the mainstream news. It's the new mantra. *Youth ministry practices are not consistently supporting a sustained faith beyond high school.*[1] For those of us who have worked with young people for decades, this news is difficult to swallow because we see God working powerfully in the lives of teenagers. In fact, we can see familiar faces forming a collage worth celebrating.

Anthony has no religious background. Because his parents feel pressured by their own religious upbringings, they want to raise Anthony without any religious baggage. They live down the street from our church but don't know anyone who goes there. Anthony admires the old, stone frame of the building and its dominating steeple. Every time his family drives by the church, he quietly prays, "God, are you in there?" As he describes it, one day God answers and beckons him inside.

I meet Anthony that day. He comes into the worship service late and sits in the back. After a polite name exchange, he says, "God told me to come here." Anticipation fills his eyes and tears roll down my checks. For the next three years, Anthony responds to God's invitation, which brings him right to Jesus. He encounters God's deep love and a community trying, even if imperfectly, to demonstrate this love to him. Anthony is part of everything—Bible studies, service to the community, and teaching children's Sunday school. If it happens at the church, Anthony is part of it. Twenty years later, Anthony continues to respond to God's invitation as a social worker caring for foster kids. Anthony defies the latest reports.

So does Cassandra. She is a lively middle schooler who is always ready to tell a funny story. As long as she can remember, her family came to the church. She knows every crevasse of the building and thinks it is a second home. Her face shines a constant smile, sometimes in delight and sometimes in mischief. In any case, her joy is part of the church's wallpaper. Then there is a messy divorce, and the secure foundation beneath her feet cracks. At first, all she does is cry. Her image of a benevolent God who gave her a happy life is gone. Poof. Over the next year, she wanders around the church as if looking for something, which she is. She is lost.

One night after youth group, a youth leader invites Cassandra to follow a simple guitar chord progression on the piano. With years of piano lessons in hand, Cassandra soon joins him leading music at youth group. There are no deep talks or heartfelt exchanges. But there is companionship as the two of them coordinate their chords. Reflecting back, Cassandra describes how learning to lead people in worship provides space to grieve, heal, and reimagine God in the messiness of life. Today, Cassandra is a pastor. She still leads worship from the piano and preaches powerful sermons full of compassion and hope amid life's disarray.

Perhaps you too can identify faces that would similarly fill a collage of young people who grow up to be maturing followers of Christ. These individuals know life's challenges, but they persistently follow Jesus. Their stories make us want to deny the reverberating news reports, because their lives testify to God's transforming work among us.

Add to this the long list of deeply committed adults who devote tremendous time, energy, and resources to young people. Over the past century this dedication has led to rapid growth in the field of youth ministry. Church and parachurch youth ministries of all stripes (some with hefty budgets) have multiplied. Youth workers are increasingly well equipped, some earning specialized undergraduate and graduate degrees. Curriculum and training events are widely available. No longer are these events primarily selling games and techniques. They also offer deep insight and prompt thoughtful and entrepreneurial ministry initiatives. Scholars in theology and the social sciences publish in academic journals focused on youth ministry. All of this sounds like clear, even measurable, success. With our collage of faces in hand, we want to reject the recent reports.

Unfortunately, there is a second collage filled with important faces. Here we see young people, many now adults, for whom we had every hope. They had transforming encounters with Jesus, participated in lots of programs and events, and now appear disinterested at best, antagonistic at worst. Sadly, this second collage confirms the reports. Eduardo is front and center in my collage.

Like Cassandra, Eduardo's parents raise him in the church, and he comes to everything we do. He has the gift of evangelism and brings packs of friends to youth group. Eduardo loves to tell people about Jesus' love. He is a deep thinker and easily engages in nonthreatening conversations about faith and life with teachers and classmates at school. Moved by Jesus' compassion, he reaches out to high school friends who live on the margins. People's lives are touched by his thoughtfulness and care. Eduardo inspires us all.

Then he goes to college and never looks back. Eduardo decides that the people at youth group have encountered Jesus, but he really has not. It was all just a phase. Christianity is no longer on his radar. The news reports are talking about Eduardo—and Ava.

As a teenager, Ava has a quiet presence as if she is taking it all in. Ava chooses small groups over the big events. She wants close friends and authentic relationships. The same personality traits show up in her faith. Ava loves to pray. She prays for her friends, for our troubled world, and to hear God's voice. During her senior year, Ava's dad is diagnosed with pancreatic cancer and dies within four months. We walk every step of the road with Ava, especially the dark months of grief.

Somewhere along this agonizing journey, Ava stops praying. Today her Twitter feed is filled with links to articles or posts that mock Christianity. Her real encounters with God now live in a history she denies. Ava validates the reports.

Even with our collages filled with maturing Christians and youth ministry's measurable successes, the reports confirm, at least in part, what we know to be true: *Youth ministry practices are not consistently supporting faith beyond high school graduation.*

It is like we are standing at the edge of cliff overlooking a ravine. We have resource-loaded backpacks and arrive at the scene committed for the long haul, but there is no bridge to get across. Often we are left feeling defeated and even blamed. Why is there such a deep divide between our increased effort, devotion, and resources, and numbers of young people leaving the church behind?

PLENTY OF SOLUTIONS

We don't lack for solutions. In fact, youth workers are at their best when we need creative problem solving. I see four models among the present solutions: the physician, the archaeologist, the engineer, and the coach. First, some tackle the problem like physicians who hope to identify the illness. This group stays on top of recent social science research to determine key problems or vulnerabilities. Once discovered, they write a prescription in light of the data. This approach helps adults know what to avoid, stop, or supplement.

The second model is similarly tied to the data but functions more like an archaeologist. Instead of looking for what is wrong, they dig around for what is right. They ask questions such as, When young people maintain a maturing faith after high school, what are the contributing factors? Upon discovery of hidden artifacts, creative programming seeks to make the findings relevant.

A third model involves acting like an engineer. Since present practices in youth ministry appear ineffective, this group is solution oriented. The situation requires ingenuity so they can remodel youth ministries around a specific theory or ideal. Rebuilding from the ground up is the task.

Finally, there are those who choose the coach model. They declare the problem is not what we are doing but a lack of training. This group blows a whistle and calls us to action. Increasing our effort, ability, and commitment based on what we already know will ensure we win the game.

Each of these models is helpful and offers us valuable insight and resources. We do need to diagnose the problem, discover key artifacts, redesign ministries, and train according to what we know. Yet each also has inherent problems.

MELON CONSUMPTION

The physician and archaeologist depend so much on the data that the social science lens takes precedence over the theological. Here's an exaggerated example. Imagine researchers demonstrate that young people who eat melon on Tuesdays are among those with sustained faith. In response, ministries focus on increasing melon consumption. Small groups move to Tuesdays. They serve melon balls, melon smoothies, and melon pizza. The benefits of melon become the focus of leader training. Parents receive melon samples to take home. Books about creative ways to integrate melon eating on Tuesdays line the youth worker's bookshelf. Budgets shift to allow for the purchase of large quantities of melon. Curriculum is available and can be downloaded weekly. Here's the problem. Did anyone ask what eating melon on Tuesdays has to do with Christianity?

Melon eating might just align with the faith, but the gospel is likely to shape why or how we eat melon. Yes, a silly example. But I bet you can fill in the blank with popular data findings we grab as if they solve everything. The information we gain from the data is important, but decisions based on this information must undergo theological reflection.[2] What we learn from the social sciences needs to become a point of reference for us to imagine the faith in our day, rather than adopting the information without regard to our theological convictions.

Additionally, the physician and archaeologist tend to ignore the postmodern emphasis on context, the specific setting we all live in. When we follow the goal of modernity and try to universalize answers, we miss the uniqueness of the particular. For example, if we place every leaf we see in the category "leaves," we show what is common among all leaves. There is truth to this since most grow on trees or bushes and fall to the ground in autumn. But if you have ever seen New England in the fall, you know this minimizes the brilliant array of colors among the leaves. To put leaves in one category diminishes the brilliant yellow of a hickory, the vibrant red of a sugar maple, and the earthy orange of a white oak. Similarly, the physician and archaeologist look for answers that morph into a universalizing answer. We already know that one-size-fits-all programs do not work and can potentially be destructive. The best program rises out of the specific community rather than being imposed on the community.

The ingenuity of engineers inspires us. When they remodel ministries according to new theories, this generates hope and excitement. Yet often new models don't take past achievements seriously. Instead, time-tested youth ministry principles collapse amid the demolition rather than being integrated into the remodeled ministry. Important factors such as the prevalence of adolescent subculture, the importance of age-appropriate learning, or the variety of church traditions are often forgotten.

Unfortunately, the coach's rally cry, although genuine, is hard to hear and feels a bit like denial when real faces continue to fill our collages. Yes, we have done many things really well in youth ministry, and there is much to celebrate. Yet the anxiety-producing labels filling our newsfeeds require attention: *the dones* are simply fed up with Christianity, *the nones* claim no religious affiliation, and *the spiritual but not religious* welcome the divine but have no use for the institutional church.[3] Each label represents a family member or friend we care about. For some of us, these labels are us. Simply trying harder or committing more resources is not the solution.

A CALL FOR THEOLOGICAL REFLECTION

Amid the present solutions, other areas of research are taking precedence over the theological. When this happens, churches end up eating melon on Tuesdays and miss the opportunity to reflect on our theology and its influence on ministry practices. How might our beliefs be shaping, maybe even causing, the worrisome reports? There are multiple theological questions to be asked once we begin to utilize a theological lens. I will focus on just one.

Decreased participation in the local church after high school is a primary measurement accompanying the declaration that youth ministry practices aren't consistently fostering a sustained faith. Yet *do we believe being part of the church is critical to Christian life?* When Camille or Marcus shows up at youth group, we ultimately hope to foster in them a faith that can flourish into adulthood. I feel confident you agree with me here. Yet what is the church's role in this vision? More specifically, *what is the relationship between the person and the community of faith? How have we understood this relationship in youth ministry practices, and how should we?*

Before exploring this further, a few clarifications are in order. First, the questions I just asked are intrinsically theological. Meaning, I am curious about the relationship between God, Christ's church, and the Spirit's work among people. As soon as we seek to understand God and our relationship with God, we have stepped into the theological.

What is the relationship between a young person (and surely all Christians) and the community of faith?

My approach joins with the theological turn in youth ministry. As Andy Root and Kenda Dean declare, we have spent so long "justifying our ministries for their sociological, educational or therapeutic usefulness."[4] A movement is underway that more intentionally reflects theologically on youth ministry practices.[5] The following chapters include other areas of research such as history, psychology, education, and sociology, but I examine them in service of one core theological question: What is the relationship between a young person (and surely all Christians) and the community of faith?

Second, I am asking a question that belongs to a specific area in theological studies called ecclesiology. Ecclesiology is a branch of theology concerned with the church's nature (what is the church?) and function (what does the church do?). You may be reading this book as a Baptist, Presbyterian, Pentecostal, Catholic, Methodist, or any of the nondenominational streams flowing from the Christian river. Your community has a distinct way of understanding what the church is (nature) and what the church is called to do (function).

I am giving a presentation at a conference on this topic. I explain that we face an ecclesiological question that spans the different Christian denominations. A man sitting in the back quickly points out the impossibility of this task. He contends that our ecclesiology always comes out of a distinct theological tradition. A Presbyterian view of the church should be different from a Southern Baptist or a Roman Catholic perspective.[6] Surely the main premise of his objection is accurate. Yet adults within Christianity's distinct streams are trying to care for young people, reading the same discouraging reports, and swimming in similar cultural waters. Rising out of these waters is a specific question riding an ecclesiological wave that spans Christianity: What is the relationship between the person and the community of faith?

REFRAMING

My hope is to provide an additional frame to the current models. Reframing what we presently see and paying attention to it is a difficult task. It's like looking at an optical illusion with two simultaneous perspectives. Maybe you have seen the black-and-white picture that portrays both an older woman and a younger woman? It takes effort to focus our eyes to see beyond our first perception, letting the lines and shapes bend to form a new image. Sometimes when the new frame appears, it does so suddenly, and we can only see it for a moment. But with time and effort, this new frame becomes more natural and takes less effort to see. A sustained look through a new frame is then possible.

We already have a dominant frame in place. This frame generally utilizes social-science research to examine why young people are leaving church behind. We should anticipate that reframing the situation as a *theological inquiry* will take time as our eyes adjust to this new way of seeing. We know this situation warrants our efforts because something significant is at stake—the lives of young people and, in some ways, the Christian faith itself. Seeing through a new frame holds exciting possibilities. As a first step, let's examine the waters of our culture.

SWIMMING IN DEEP CULTURAL WATERS

The waters of mobility: Community as voluntary. I live in a small New Hampshire town that in some ways belongs to another era. We love the town green behind town hall where we enjoy winter visits from Santa riding atop a firetruck, spring egg hunts, summer concerts, and fall pumpkin lighting. The white clapper-board church sits across the street nestled next to the town elementary school. It's picturesque, but does not necessarily represent twenty-first century life. The century-old town structure represents a time when community was integral to daily life. Whether you liked your neighbor or not, you depended on one another and looked out for each other's kids. There's no need to romanticize this era—it was also full of deep problems. But there was something distinct about the community that is less prevalent today.

Sociologist Robert Putnam is one of many who concludes that community is changing in American society.[7] In fact, extensive data reveals ways in which we are increasingly disconnected from one another. The social structures that previously provided identity and belonging are disappearing and result in a loss of social capital, which include dependable social networks such as the PTA, churches, local coffee shops, and, yes, events on my town green. Community was more often a given in society. I lend you my snowblower, and you invite me over when we lose electricity. There was a give and take to these relationships—reciprocation—because people more readily saw themselves as citizens participating in their neighborhoods, towns, and society.

With increased mobility and economic development (among other factors), we simply have other options. We are less obliged to one another because there are alternatives. Rather than community including dependable, social networks, community today is voluntary because we choose the communities we belong to. Three decades ago Robert Wuthnow studied what he called the small group phenomena—from support groups like AA to small groups in churches and synagogues—to determine the nature of these community connections.[8] People expressed the importance of these communities in their lives based on the support they received. This also meant that when their personal needs ceased to be met, people went in search of other communities.

When satisfaction is the basis of community, personal choice often trumps long-standing commitment. Self and personal needs become the center and determining factor for a community. Does this sound familiar? If the church doesn't meet my or my family's needs, we find another community. This is not a declaration that people are selfish by intent, but a recognition that people in our churches—this is us— understand community as voluntary and this shaped our way of being together in our churches.

The waters of specialization: Churches as service providers. Mocking people's belief in God is a hobby for Dr. Gregory House, the main character on the popular television drama *House.* In one episode, a young couple travels a long way to see House because of his reputation as a medical genius. The woman has a life-threatening heart problem and no doctor has been able to figure out what's wrong. Throughout the episode the woman persists in her belief that God will help her even amid House's condescending taunts and challenges. During a risky angioplasty procedure, House discovers she was born with a significant structural problem to her heart. This is the evidence House needs. God is not the loving deity she presumes, for "A human wouldn't screw up that big."

Pointing out the shortcomings of religious belief is great fodder for stand-up comedy or poignant moments in a series like *House.* Religion has not always been perceived like this. In fact, the role of religion has changed significantly throughout history. Before the Age of Enlightenment birthed the modern era, Christianity had a defined and respected role in society. Picture medieval Europe's cathedral dominating the city square with its spire extending toward the heavens. Visible throughout the city, this massive edifice provides a point of orientation for everyone who lives there. The sheer size of the cathedral compared to its surroundings demonstrates Christianity's influence and authority in this place. Religion as a "cathedral" influenced education, politics, and even science. (This is not to say the influence was always positive.) Now compare the cathedral to a contemporary storefront church. Unlike the cathedral, the storefront rents space in order to gain influence. To be noticed, this church needs an eye-catching sign and a visually appealing website. Programs are created to attract people, and sermons must capture attention. Instead of permeating all aspects of society like the cathedral, the storefront church has to create influence.

Sociologist Niklas Luhmann helps us understand what is behind this shift. Why has religion's role in society changed so dramatically? His theory, called social differentiation, describes a significant change in relationship among the various sectors of society.[9] Luhmann suggests that with modernity comes an increasingly complex society. Each sector must now work to establish its distinct identity and purpose in order to survive. This results in each sector developing and making known their specialized roles as if marking their territory and vying for attention. Each sector must ask, What do we offer? Religion is not immune.

The storefront church must compete for a role in society. Think about the implications of this. Communities of faith change from being authorities with a given societal role to religious specialists peddling a product to meet religious needs. This sociological position shapes how churches attract members, seek converts, or explain the faith. Ultimately, in modern societies churches must compete for attention as the specialized service providers of religion who offer a unique product: spirituality.

Pitting science against religion, as Dr. House does with a conviction that the two cannot coexist, is an outgrowth of this change. The doctor heals the body, and the church heals the soul. When House's patient prays for God to heal her, she dares to take religion into medicine's territory. The cathedral morphs into the storefront church. Churches become service providers alongside society's other sectors. Specialization is one characteristic of the cultural waters that all American churches swim in. As we tread water, a third characteristic emerges.

> **Communities of faith change from being authorities with a given societal role to religious specialists peddling a product to meet religious needs.**

The waters of commodification: Consuming as a condition. On road trips, my family looks forward to crossing through Pennsylvania, otherwise known as the land of WaWa stores. They have a great sandwich bar with hundreds of options to choose from just by tapping one of many computer screens. Adding chipotle sauce to the list is simply brilliant. The coffee options seem limitless and the candy aisle puts Willy Wonka to shame. We love the WaWa stop because we get to pick out exactly what we want.

Everywhere we go, from health insurance companies to banks to clothing stores, specialized sectors appeal to our personal needs, hoping to gain allegiance. And we like it. I enjoy being able to reserve the reclining seat in the back of the movie theater. I am not only a coffee snob (I drink Dunkin' though; I live in the northeast), I proudly call myself a water snob (Come on—you know there is a difference between Dasani and Aquafina). Preference. Choice. Desire. I grew up with Sesame Street twice a day (the same episode), and my children have four twenty-four-hour Disney channels on their personal, handheld screens. It should be of no surprise to see the Christian message also morph into a commodity to consume just like a specialty sandwich.[10] We are swimming, and maybe drowning, in a consumer culture.

Theologian Vincent Miller defines consumer culture as "cultural habits of use and interpretation that are derived from the consumption of commodified cultural objects."[11] A commodity is something that can be bought and sold in the marketplace. Commodification means giving something a market value (turning it into a commodity) that actually cannot be bought or sold, such as love, beauty, or freedom.[12] An advertisement for outdoor clothing sells its product not because it promises to keep you warm in the winter but by appealing to your sense of adventure. Marketers sell us a toy not only for fun but because it promises to bring families together. The shoes we buy bring joy, and phones provide community.

Katherine Turpin describes the market's power as a "vocational script" young people (and even adults) build their lives around. Even if they can logically identify the shallowness and inaccuracy of these messages, young people are still devoted followers.[13] My son comes home from preschool one day asking to buy a pair of shoes with that "swish" on the side. I ask why. "Because they will make me run fast," he says with a glimmer in his eye. Nike stole his heart at age four. His allegiance to their advertising pledge to increase his athletic performance persists even as he is old enough to articulate the fallacy.

Miller contends that the pervasiveness of consumer culture acts like a lens through which we reinterpret the Christian faith. It's as if we put on a pair of glasses and everything we see changes form. Religious symbols, beliefs, and practices intended to describe God's transcendence, help us encounter mystery, or remind us of other people's needs transform into commodities for our personal consumption. Potentially, we exchange an identity based on the selfless love of Christ for a Christian identity of personal satisfaction.

A number of years ago a parody of the church went viral. People with various backgrounds and life situations drive up to an intercom to place their church order. The welcoming voice on the intercom announces, "We get your order right the first time, every time, all the time, on time, until the end of time. How can we feed you today?"[14] A young mom asks for rainbow goldfish crackers and no VeggieTales songs, which annoyingly get stuck in her head. Sermons to make him "feel good" are on the order of an angry man. And surely, he adds, these come from the New Testament because the Old Testament stories are about an angry God. Every person has an opinion about the music style, quality, and quantity. Requests go on—length of sermon, time spent standing, friendliness of greeters, children's programming, and shape of the communion crackers.

We laugh because the clip points to our own experiences. And we laugh because this reality is ludicrous and deserves laughter. No one needs to tell us that shopping for a church based on our personal needs is inconsistent with the gospel. And yet we swim in waters where preference, choice, and desire are our oxygen. We even fear that if our churches don't fulfill people's desires, they will cease to exist. Maybe our fears are correct. As I write this, please note that my finger is not pointing outward at the others who are doing this. I am pointing at myself too, and the churches I call home. Are we reducing "the image of the invisible God, the firstborn over all creation" (Colossians 1:15) to be only *my* Jesus and *my* Savior? We are swimming in consumer waters and find ourselves conditioned to consume.

Swimming with the current: Churches and the gospel package. I am driving down the road on a summer day and pass the local congregational church. A huge, colorful banner announcing Vacation Bible School fills the front lawn. As I turn the corner and approach the town's Catholic parish, my jaw drops. There it is, exactly the same banner.

Apparently, a popular Christian publisher markets their VBS curriculum across the theological spectrum. The Protestant and Catholic versions aren't identical, but the core of the content is the same. Jesus loves you, Jesus is with you, Jesus died for you, and Jesus calls you. Maybe this is a trend toward Christian unity around the essence of the Christian faith. Or maybe this illustrates the conflation of historic Protestant and Catholic teachings. I fear it is the latter. In order to swim in this culture, churches, now religious specialists, must develop a product that can be sold to the consumer who understands community as voluntary. The result is what I call the "gospel package," a minimal version of the Christian message tailored to satisfy personal desire.

Personalization of the gospel is prevalent.[15] The Christian story morphs from a story about a community into a story about me and for me. First-person pronouns saturate our descriptions of God's activity in the life, death, and resurrection of Christ, leaving us with a small gospel about Jesus who died just for me. This creates an image of God who is always on my side and always working for my best interest. We judge worship gatherings based on feeling fed by good sermons or how it facilitated our personal encounter with God. Our service to others finds meaning not solely in caring for others but because it makes us feel good. And ministries, including youth ministries, evolve around the primary purpose of connecting individuals to Jesus. This gospel package is prevalent, to varying degrees, across the Christian traditions. I am not saying this message is inaccurate. Surely the gospel is personal. I am saying that it is an incomplete message. The gospel is much bigger than *me* and my personal religious experience.

After reading this, very few people would affirm the theological premise of the gospel package with self clearly as the central focus. But we know it well. For it is the package we are buying and selling. The package did not design itself; we, the church, created it in order to navigate a society where religion needs a specialty to create influence, communities have shifted from a given to voluntary, and the force of consumer culture demands personalization. The need for theological reflection on the well-known gospel package is the dilemma we presently face with our collages in hand.

2

GALLOPING MARES

THE GOSPEL WITHOUT CHRIST'S CHURCH

W E NEED TO FIND an answer to the pressing question before us instead of continuing to eat melon on Tuesdays. How should we understand the relationship between the Christian and the community of faith? I see three main answers to this question: the relationship is superfluous, supportive, or vital. Each answer includes a view of the church, an ecclesiology. In this chapter, I will briefly explain and illustrate all three views, and then critique superfluous and supportive, which I find to be insufficient. The following three chapters will cast a vision for a vital ecclesiology.

SUPERFLUOUS VIEW

Superfluous ecclesiology means the church is *un*necessary for the Christian to mature and grow as a follower of Jesus Christ. Sometimes this answer is a result of bad experiences in the church. A person deems active participation in the church as unessential because the community just can't get out of its own way. Or maybe the church is consistently embroiled in conflict and division. Because a person has negative experiences with the church as an institution, it is seen as a barrier to maturing faith. Thus, it is easy to conclude the church is superfluous for a Christian. For others, this answer is more foundational. Even at its best moments the church itself is not ultimately the goal. Instead, the greater vision is for individuals to have a personal relationship with Jesus Christ. When the relationship between the church and the Christian is superfluous, it might look something like the following example.

> Jeff is glad it is Sunday morning. He can sleep late and spend time reading the Bible and praying. He stopped going to church a few months ago for two reasons. First, soccer and school keep him very busy, and he decided that his personal relationship with God is what matters. So he prioritizes spending time alone with God. There's only so much time in the day, and he wants to put God first. Second, churches seem to be distracted by other things like making rules, judging people, or disagreeing about silly things. Jeff feels he is doing fine with his spiritual life and avoids these distractions in order to go deeper with God on his own.

SUPPORTIVE VIEW

A supportive ecclesiology assumes the church is uniquely called to support a Christian's maturing faith. Ministries, Bible studies, community groups, and service activities all exist to help people develop a vibrant faith. Worship gatherings act as a conduit for the person to give praise and thanksgiving to God, to confess sin, to embrace forgiveness, to receive instruction, and to seek God's help. Music plays an essential role as lyrics draw a person into intimate communion with God. When a person's faith ceases to be enriched by the church's programs and activities, this warrants searching for a new community that will better support spiritual nourishment. A supportive relationship between the Christian and the church looks like Jennifer's experience.

Jennifer loves her church and takes advantage of all opportunities to grow in her relationship with God. She goes to a Bible study, youth group, and most Sunday school classes. She doesn't attend the worship service very often, because she connects more with God when she goes to the youth programs. Jennifer's youth worker suggests meeting with a group of friends before school to hold each other accountable, and she is going to find time for this because it will help her go deeper in her faith. She even goes to the nursing home once a week—it feels so good to serve others. Jennifer is thankful for her church and youth group because the supportive environment helps her grow closer to Christ.

VITAL VIEW

A person's relationship with the community of faith is vital to a maturing faith in Christ. In fact, there is no such thing as a solo Christian, for to be a Christian is to join with fellow Christ-followers. Certainly, there are examples of people throughout history and in our present day who live vibrant lives of faith when barred from Christian fellowship by oppressive regimes or forced isolation. But these are exceptions. God's movement in the world includes forming a people, a building, a temple— we are the body of Christ. When a person's relationship with the community is vital, the church carries out the dual task of nurturing an individual's relationship with God and the community's relationship with each other. A vital relationship may look like the following example.

Chloe has been going to the same church for three years and is active in the youth program. She also attends the worship service almost every Sunday for three reasons. First, when the church prays and sings together, she feels her faith strengthen. Sometimes life is difficult, and she feels sustained by others during these times. Other times her faith feels firm, which she declares confidently hoping others will hear and be encouraged. Second, Chloe is part of a small group that cares for and learns from each

other. They serve at the local soup kitchen because they are trying
to love their neighbors. Sometimes the group has disagreements,
but they take these opportunities to work on loving each other.
After all, you can't learn patience without being with people who
drive you crazy. Third, Chloe is a gifted artist. The leader of the
special needs ministry at church found out and asked Chloe to
teach art to the kids. Chloe now enjoys visiting them once a
month and teaching basic art skills. It's exciting to know that she
has something to contribute to the church. Chloe experiences
her faith in Christ as intimately connected to this community.

SUPERFLUOUS IS NOT A FEASIBLE OPTION

There have been seasons in my life when viewing the church as superfluous to my faith was rather appealing. It seems churches have the
unique capacity to breed discord. I suspect you understand. Maybe Bonhoeffer is right: our expectations that Christian communities should
somehow be more than what they are—the gathering of those in desperate need of Christ's forgiveness—is the source of our disillusionment.[1]
Alas, the author of Hebrews speaks loudly to a superfluous ecclesiology.
The author is concerned about people among them who are in in danger
of drifting away from the faith (Hebrews 2:1). A remedy is put forward.
"Let us consider . . . not giving up meeting together, as some are in the
habit of doing, but encouraging one another—all the more as you see
the Day approaching" (Hebrews 10:24-25). There is an underlying fear
in the author's response. If these Christ-followers stop joining with
other believers, they would be in danger of abandoning the faith. This
plea does not come out of a developed ecclesiology but from experience.

People of faith need to be in fellowship with others and "encourage
one another daily" (Hebrews 3:13). *Is a superfluous relationship between
the Christian and the church even a viable option?*

"Spiritual but not religious" is another label used to describe the
increasing number of people who no longer participate in churches but

maintain an active faith.[2] Some justify this group by saying it is a unique phase of spiritual development for emerging adults. A person needs to separate from the institutional faith (the religious) in order to personally appropriate faith (the spiritual). The National Study of Youth and Religion, the largest study to date on the religious attitudes of young people, refutes this and names it the myth of "internal without external religion."[3] Their findings indicate that those who demonstrate strong faith commitment regularly attend worship services. Similarly, those with low faith commitment decrease in worship attendance. The conclusion: private religion is less sustainable as a young person transitions into adulthood. This validates the author's fear in Hebrews, and the church being superfluous to a maturing Christian is not defensible.

And yet we are drawn to this idea. In 2012, Jefferson Bethke produced a video titled "Why I Hate Religion, but Love Jesus."[4] The video went viral and in just a few weeks had eighteen million hits. Bethke's words struck a chord with the Christian world. He contrasts religion, the institutionalized church, to Jesus. Through aphorisms and rhythmic stanzas, he defines the church as a distorter of the true teachings of Jesus. "Religion puts you in bondage, but Jesus sets you free." As you can imagine, the video produced a lot of media chatter from *Christianity Today* to the *New York Times*. People were critiquing his thin declarations about the church being a "human invention" and setting up a false dichotomy between following Jesus versus participating in the church. Eventually, Bethke admitted his message needed clarification. The relationship between a Christian and the church simply cannot be superfluous or unnecessary. At the very least, Christians need others to support their faith journey. A superfluous ecclesiology is not feasible.

SUPPORTIVE IS A PARTIAL VISION

What about the supportive view? Should Christians see the church's role as supporting personal faith? There is something familiar about Jennifer in the earlier scenario, is there not? Jennifer appears to be doing all the things we would hope for in a young person who is a maturing Christ-follower. She is a faithful youth group attendee; she goes to Bible study and even Sunday school (imagine that). Jennifer responds well to her youth worker's prompting by forming an accountability group, and she feels good about serving in a nursing home. Her church is providing so many opportunities for Jennifer to grow in her faith. Maybe we could throw in a mentoring program or help Jennifer better craft her quiet time, but as it is, this seems like the ideal experience we want for young people. Or is it?

Note the relationship between Jennifer and her church. The church's purpose is to support Jennifer's faith. Is this really all a church is supposed to do? Is this really the ultimate aim of a youth ministry? A supportive ecclesiology like this contains a partial vision. It is true in some respects and not true in others. Partial vision is vulnerable to misinterpretation.

At age four my daughter fearlessly faces the ocean waves. She stands before them with determination, daring them to topple her, and laughing joyfully as they meet this challenge time and again. But at age five, my daughter avoids the same waves. She apprehensively plays at the surf's edge, clinging to a boogie board, and peering nervously into the dark ocean waters. What changed? At some point in between her ocean visits, she hears a friend talk about seahorses. She knows the words *sea* and *horse*, and apparently her imagination fills in the blank. The ocean is teeming with giant galloping mares! My daughter has partial knowledge; she only knows what *sea* and *horse* mean. This is enough to make sense of each individual word and create meaning, but her understanding remains partial. This deeply affects her vision of the ocean.

Rather than just being inaccurate, a partial perspective is not complete or full. To say the church should support a Christian's personal relationship with Christ is true—but partial. The problem with partial understanding is that we might interpret the ocean depths of faith full of galloping mares and miss the fullness of what

God intends. Partial spirituality is what pastoral theologian David Augsburger sees. Drawing on his Anabaptist tradition, Augsburger defines three participants in our spiritual life: God, self, and others.[5] We have the option of engaging with one, two, or all three. Augsburger makes a bold assertion. He contends that because Roman Catholic and Protestant traditions focus on personal redemption, they genuinely engage only two of the three participants. Why? Because we follow in the footsteps of St. Augustine, who claimed, "For Thou hast made us for Thyself and our hearts are restless till they rest in Thee."[6] In this line of thinking, the Christian story prioritizes God and self. Augsburger contends this makes God a divine reference point outside of self, beckoning people toward wholeness through a personal, relational encounter with God. "I know true self as I know God."[7]

And who are others? According to Augsburger, other people have two roles. First, others are an additional benefit to the primary relationship between God and self. This means their role is to support the faith of the individual person. Sound familiar? Second, others are recipients of the care we offer out of obedience to God. Caring for others is a consequence or obligation. We care for others because God says so. Others are not integral, necessary, or essential to my life as a Christian. In a consumer culture, others easily become a nice tool or added benefit used to meet my spiritual needs.

Although Augsburger's characterization of the Roman Catholic and Protestant traditions may be a bit sweeping, he rightly questions minimizing other people. Is the God-self relationship always primary or separate from the self-other relationship? If so, the church's role is only to support the individual Christian's faith. If not, this reveals that a supportive ecclesiology is a partial vision.

Yet the gospel package continues to affirm the church's role as supportive. Imagine the scene. Ten thousand people gather for a worship experience. Eyes close and hands reach upward. The lights are low except the dim glow around the stage as the musicians crescendo to the chorus "Lord, I give You my heart, I give You my soul, I live for You alone."[8] I don't wish to demean such sacred moments, only to ask a question: Why are the other people present? Why is it necessary to be with ten thousand other Christians in order to sing this song? The words are a personal prayer, a first-person singular declaration of *my* submission to God. I know the answer; remember I am an actor in this drama too. *It is inspiring to hear so many other people declare their commitment to God. Such experiences support my personal relationship with God.* True? Yes. This is an example of the ecclesiology inherent to the gospel package. The church's role is to support the faith of individual Christians. And when the church does not do this, it's time to church hop and shop.

A clarification is in order. I am not saying that worship gatherings are bad or worship songs should not be sung using personal pronouns. Surely the church is charged to urge individuals toward greater maturity. The author of Hebrews admonishes the people because, like infants, they still need milk rather than eating the solid food of the mature. Instead, they are to "move . . . forward to maturity" (Hebrews 6:1). The church should support our Christian growth. But is this the only defining mark of our relationship with the Christian community? The worship experience scenario, an illustration of the dominant gospel package, says it is.

YOUTH MINISTRIES AS SUPPORTIVE ECCLESIOLOGY

In our most recent history the dominant youth ministry philosophies and practices[9] already have an answer to the pressing question, What is a Christian's relationship to the church? The church should support a young person's growing faith. In the scenario about Jennifer, it is easy to see how a common youth ministry paradigm holds to a supportive ecclesiology. We build programs and offer great opportunities to support faith. One writer takes individualization to the extreme. Just as Paul and Jesus customized the gospel for the different people, he says, "We absolutely must *individualize*, *customize*, and *personalize* our youth ministries."[10] Instead of people being transformed into the image of Christ, this proclamation asks Christ to transform for each person's needs. An unexamined supportive ecclesiology is contributing to the reality we presently face.

There is another contributor beyond youth ministry programs. I hear a supportive ecclesiology in our words. People use a variety of phrases to describe their desire to invite the next generation into the Christian faith. Some use relational language such as "sharing the faith" and others use authoritative phrases stemming from a parent's responsibility to "train a child in the way to go." Most commonly, church leaders and parents use the phrase "passing on the faith." I hear it everywhere. During worship gatherings, pastors pray for young people to be secure in the faith *passed* to them. Church leaders hire consultants to find ways to increase their effectiveness at *passing* the faith. Parents quickly give time and money to ensure a son or daughter owns the faith they *passed*. This phrase sells books. Researchers Merton Strommen and Richard Hardel propose a new model for youth and family ministry in a book titled *Passing On the Faith*.[11] In her influential book *Godbearing Life*, practical theologian Kenda Dean says, "Godbearing youth ministry embraces all the formal . . . and informal . . . ways of *passing on faith*."[12]

We perpetuate a supportive ecclesiology when we talk about our desire to "pass on the faith" to young people. I am not criticizing our intent behind the use of this phrase. We easily pass on recommendations about less important parts of life. My son can't wait for me to hear the unique sound of Pentatonix, an a cappella group, and I think everyone needs to see *The Way* with Martin Sheen. Our faith is far more important than these things. Something would be dreadfully wrong if we did not possess a desire to share our faith with others. Certainly, the impulse to pass on our faith to young people is noble and right, not to mention called for in the Scriptures (1 Corinthians 15:3). My concern is for how this particular phrase, "passing the faith," *functions* in our context.

Postmodern philosophers remind us that language is never static. Words are in a dynamic relationship with their environment. This means that our social context gives added meaning to our words. For example, in the middle of the 2008-2009 financial crises in America, many were describing the situation as analogous to an earthquake such as "the ground is shifting" or "our foundations are crumbling." Then on January 12, 2010, a massive earthquake devastated the people and land of Haiti. Afterward, one news commentator rightly received a great deal of criticism for continuing to use earthquake metaphors to describe the financial crisis. The words took on new meaning as we saw lives in Haiti lost or devastated. Because the social context changed, the meaning of the words and how listeners understood them had also changed.

Conversely, words can give meaning to our experiences. I recently spoke at a youth retreat and described myself as adventure challenged. I am the kind of person who loves the idea of adventure but struggles with the execution. The idea of snorkeling in clear water and watching colorful parades of fish is thrilling. Putting on the mask and trying to breathe through a pipe produces claustrophobic panic. It is exhilarating to imagine flying above the trees on a zip line. But my friends can testify to the lengthy time I recently spent sitting frozen at the top of the wire, rendering me unable to take the plunge. I confessed to the group gathered on this retreat that I am adventure challenged. A funny thing happened. The kids took the term and applied it to their experiences. It was February in New Hampshire, and the wind chill was below zero, not ideal even for winter sports. One girl described the sledding hill as "No place for the adventure challenged." A guy urged another to face him in a game of foosball, jesting, "Unless you are adventure challenged."

Words can shape our experiences just as our experiences give meaning to our words. How does the phrase "passing on the faith" shape how we understand and carry out youth ministries? Does the way we speak affirm a supportive ecclesiology? I think it does.

Let's compare the meaning of the phrase "passing the faith" in two social contexts. In the New Testament, the passing phrase is used in 1 Corinthians 15:3: "What I received I passed on to you." Paul uses these words to connect himself to the apostles and demonstrate the authority of the message he is preaching, "Christ died for our sins." In Paul's time, showing how authority was passed from one person to another validated the person (and subsequently the message). Imagine batons passed between runners in a relay race. Similarly, the words *received* and *passed* in this passage describe the literal transfer of authority from one to another. The genealogies of Genesis and Matthew have a similar function. In this sense, Christians today are still called to *pass* the authoritative message to others, including younger generations.

Does the passing phrase carry the same meaning in our context?[13] Passing and receiving seem more closely tied to the service industry than to the transfer of an author-itative message. Imagine walking into a local coffee shop. The sales-person greets you with a smile, asks

How does the phrase "passing on the faith" shape how we understand and carry out youth ministries?

for your order, takes your money, and hands you the perfect cup of coffee. The exchange ends with another smile and wish for a good day. Both you and the salesperson play defined roles in this transaction. Yet what if you enjoy the coffee so much you want the salesperson to have the same experience? You offer to come behind the counter and fix her a cup. Such a gesture may receive a chuckle, but if you were persistent, the manager would show you the door. The salesperson's role is to be a service provider by passing you the product, and the customer's role is to receive the product passed. This is our social context. The phrase "passing the faith" takes on distinct meaning for us.

There are two implications. First, passing language designates roles consistent with a service provider: (1) the person passing the service, and (2) the person receiving the service. Applied to youth ministry, adults pass the faith, and young people receive the faith. What is a young person's relationship with the church here? Supportive. Adults (passers) support and young people (receivers) are supported. (For the grammar geek, note the active verb attached to the adult action in the sentence and the passive verb used for the young person.) These roles are present in Paul's social context as well. But these roles have a purpose attached to the words; *passing* shows authority in order to validate the message.

Second, passing language also implies a product, like a specialty coffee, that fits in a neat box called "the Christian faith." The church's rich and diverse tradition, meaning the ongoing search to know and understand the movement of God, is evidence that the Christian faith includes a continuing dialogue across history and cultures. Christians have always and will always seek to discern God's activity, past, present, and future. This does not mean that our

> **Passing language also implies a product, like a specialty coffee, that fits in a neat box called "the Christian faith."**

discerning always hits the mark. Simply stated, Christians get things right, and Christians get things wrong. Our varied history reveals this. There is no final version of the Christian faith to *pass*; instead, we join with a dynamic tradition.

This does not mean everything is relative. Neither do I mean truth is only subjective. There is a unifying core of the Christian message: redemption of all through the life, death, resurrection, and anticipated return of Jesus Christ (Colossians 1:15-20). Our greatest hope for young people is that we will invite them into this ongoing dialogue, with the Bible and our historical creeds and confessions in hand, as they seek to make sense of faith and life.

In our social context, passing language does not pose an invitation to young people. In fact, it works against this hope. Young people are not just passive recipients of the faith like in the service industry, and adults are more than passers. The Christian faith cannot be passed like a product, even though we try to with the gospel package. This is a supportive ecclesiology. We can perpetuate this partial vision in our youth ministries and churches even with the words we use.

Instead, the relationship between a Christian and the church is vital. Christian faith has the greatest potential to flourish when we recognize and value this relationship. This is what I will explore in the following chapters. Join me on this journey and bring the familiar faces on your collage with you. There is hope.

3

A VITAL IDENTITY

GOD GATHERS A PEOPLE

AM CHATTING WITH SOME FRIENDS about their church's search for a
new youth minister. The last person seems to be a mismatch. She
spends tons of time with kids and forms strong relationships but lets
the administrative work slide. Liability and medical forms are out of
date, plans come together at the last minute, and poor communication frustrates parents and church leaders. Based on this experience
the church adjusts the job description. Building relationships has
been the first job responsibility, but it moves down the list in order to
prioritize administration and communication. We know how this
plays out, don't we? The next hire will be a great organizer but less
relationally adept.

This is the pendulum swing principle: we move back and forth
from one extreme to the other. We observe it at work from hiring
practices to education to research. I remember the pediatrician
telling me that my second child should not have peanut butter until
she was two. I respond quizzically because just a few years ago the

recommendation was age one. The doctor laughs and says to expect the recommendation to swing back again. Soon enough we will be giving peanut butter to infants. In part, the pendulum swing exists because we react to what is lacking in our present experience and try to correct it. When the correction is overamplified, we swing back again.

Defining the relationship between young people and the church as vital is in danger of a pendulum swing. My critique of our over-emphasis on a person's individual relationship with Christ can result in an overfocus on community. The goal of this chapter is to expand the partial vision of a supportive ecclesiology and not leave the individual relationship behind. God's love is personal, and Christ's death and resurrection reaches individuals. Young people need to experience personal salvation in Christ. The history of American youth ministry demonstrates how attention to the personal encounter with Christ drives youth ministry's development and success.[1] Let's not swing the pendulum too far and leave this great history behind. Instead, I am committed to a theology that builds on it.

Additionally, I will avoid defining community as an ideal where we are holding hands, singing "Kumbaya," and drinking Coca-Cola, which, according to the old ad campaigns, produces peace on earth. Thomas H. Groome has profoundly shaped the fields of practical theology and religious education. His generous spirit, accompanied by a delightful Irish brogue, enriched my studies at Boston College and opened my eyes to the faith community's crucial role in a Christian's life. He also frequently warned against a community pitfall that went something like this: "The reason early twentieth-century Protestant liberalism failed is because of their *sloppy agape*." His critique points to a form of love that lacks traction. We cannot just wrap our arms around each other and claim love—this is sloppy agape. An idealized, loving community is insufficient because it ignores the pervasiveness of sin and its disruption to, and often destruction of, community.

With these dangers in mind, I will outline a vital ecclesiology in the next three chapters by examining the implications of "having been raised with Christ." The author of Colossians describes how Christ's followers join with Christ's death and resurrection "having been buried with him in baptism, in which you were also raised with him through your faith in the working God, who raised him from the dead" (Colossians 2:12). Throughout these opening chapters, we read numerous variations of this pattern—we died and were raised.[2] Yet in Colossians 3:1, the author makes a sudden shift worthy of our attention. There is no mention here of having died. The focus is on being raised. The author writes, "Since, then, you have been raised with Christ, set your hearts on things above." Being "raised with Christ" is our eschatological hope (how all things will be in the end) and the direction we are facing now. This has implications for our relationships with one another. I am curious about our raised-ness. *What is the nature of our raised relationship with God and one another?* When we answer this question, we can better articulate a young person's relationship with the community now.

A NEW MISCONCEPTION

When pastors and theologians talk about the church, we often start by clearing up two common misconceptions. First, the church is not a building; rather, the church is the people. Second, the church is not an organization seeking our loyalty, for our commitment is to Christ alone. Our current situation requires a third option not on the misconception list. The church is not a service provider. As I said in chapter one, we are swimming in a culture where community is voluntary, religion is a product, and consuming is a condition. This influences how we define the church's purpose as well as our expectations of community. Me and my needs can become the starting point.

This environment makes it easy for us to perceive as well as treat the church as a service provider and for the church to take on this

identity. Yet the core meaning of *church* can never be reduced to pro-
duction or consumption. If the church's primary purpose is to meet
the spiritual needs of a person or, more often, a target group such as
young people, Christian community will always be a secondary commitment. Churches are not service providers crafting the best way to
bring Jesus (a spiritually beneficial product) to people. Likewise, youth
ministries are not service providers personalizing Jesus for young
people. Reducing the church's role to only supporting a person's relationship with Jesus Christ is a misunderstanding.

Caleb shows me the implications of this new misconception. It's
Sunday morning, and I am with a handful of kids who are considering
church membership. Immediately, I can tell some come voluntarily
and others per a par-
ent's "suggestion." I pull
out a large lump of clay,
hand everyone pieces, and

**Churches are not service providers crafting
the best way to bring Jesus (a spiritually
beneficial product) to people.**

say, "Mold this into an image that describes the church." Everyone
starts thinking with their fingers—except Caleb. Clearly, this is not
where he wants to be today. One by one everyone explains their image:
a Communion table, a heart, a cross. It's Caleb's turn. I am about to
make a joke so we can graciously move past him when he says, "This
is stupid. I am not going to play with clay. But if I did mold something,
it would be me sitting in my family's car looking out the back window
as we drive away from yet another church."

The service-provider misconception has serious implications for
young people and the church at large. It is driving a wedge between
the Christian and the community of faith by sending the message that
this relationship is ancillary. I am not saying a person's relationship is
unessential. I am saying that in isolation, it misrepresents the gospel.
We need to clear up this misconception. One of a theologian's tasks is
to retrieve and reinterpret when something is forgotten. This is one of
those moments. We need to reestablish in our day why a Christian's
relationship with the church is vital.

A people. We read many descriptions in the New Testament where Christ's encounter with an individual is personally transformative. Think of Peter, John, Martha, the Samaritan woman at the well, Paul, and the disciples on the road to Emmaus. Christ meets us personally. Yet, for the early churches, being a solo Christ-follower was incomprehensible because a Christian's identity was always shared with the community.

The prevalence of the community's shared identity is difficult to miss. We see it in the family language Paul uses in his epistles. Christ-followers are "brothers and sisters" (1 Corinthians 1:10) and adopted into God's family (Galatians 4:5-6).[3] Metaphors describing the Christian community are widespread. The church is like a body (Ephesians 1:22-23; 1 Corinthians 12:27), a nation (1 Peter 2:9), a household (1 Timothy 3:15), and a building (1 Corinthians 3:9). It makes sense that these early Christ-followers had a shared identity. Social relationships across ancient Near East cultures have what cultural anthropologists Bruce Malina and Jerome Neyrey call a group-oriented personality, where belonging to the group is more important than individuality.

Even though Western social relationships are primarily oriented toward the individual, we still know what it is like to share a group's identity. Our son grows up submerged in New England sports. (What we call a privilege, you may call a curse.) At a very young age, Mason knows he is part of the Red Sox Nation. We are on a road trip heading south to visit family when he is about seven. A low gas gauge prompts us to get off the highway in New York, and Mason's jaw drops as he surveys the scene. He is truly aghast at this strange world where people plaster Yankee symbols on cars, signs, stores, and clothes. Who are these people? And worse, would he be wearing a Yankee's shirt if he grew up here? Mason is more than a loyal fan; his *being* is bound to belonging to the Red Sox Nation. The thought of *being* something else (especially a Yankee) causes momentary disequilibrium. Belonging to a group shapes our identity; our very experience as *self* is shared with *others*. Magnify this Red Sox identity, and you get a glimpse of an early Christ-follower's self-perception as inextricably connected to the Christian community.

A people belonging to God. Any introduction to ecclesiology will undoubtedly include a description of the Greek word *ekklesia*, which is commonly translated as "church" in the New Testament. When the New Testament authors use this particular word to refer to the early Christ-followers, they are expressing something very important. Using this word demonstrates they have a self-perception as a people rather than a group of individuals. The word for church literally means "the called-out ones," and the best translation into English is "gathering" or "assembly." In the first-century Greco-Roman world, *ekklesia* is often used to describe an assembly of male citizens called together to tend to local affairs.[4] We see this usage in Acts 19:32, 39, and 41. Notice that to assemble as "citizens" also suggests a shared identity. Christ-followers are a specific, called-out group. They are a people.

Furthermore, the word translated as "church" in the New Testament also implies that they assemble by invitation, like being a guest at a wedding rather than attending a concert after purchasing a ticket.[5] Multiple times Paul uses the phrase "church of God" and emphasizes that God initiates their assembly. The people are guests by invitation, and therefore God establishes that they belong. Paul is emphasizing that they are a people belonging to God.

Theologian and professor Ellen Charry describes the greatest challenge she faces teaching ecclesiology today. Her students "cannot distinguish between the church's *belonging to us* and its *belonging to God*."[6] She says this difficulty arises out of two dominant societal models we impose on the church. The church is either a corporation like a health club where we pay a fee and reap the benefits of membership, or we perceive the church as a democratic state where we vote, obey the law, pay our taxes, and therefore should enjoy living in a peaceable society. Charry contends that neither of these models adequately defines the church because each relates membership with benefits that belong to us. Instead, we belong to the church. It does not belong to us. As Charry says, "We don't make it. It makes us."[7] This is identity. The early Christ-followers did not gather by sheer will or based on a shared commitment, even if these were in the mix. Belonging to God simply as an individual was inconceivable. Their *essence* and *being* were shared. To be a Christian was to be a people belonging to God.

Linked to Israel. In addition, using the word we translate as "church" links the early Christ-followers directly to the nation of Israel as Abraham's descendants (Genesis 12). Around the third century BC, Jewish scholars translated the Old Testament from Hebrew into Greek, which is called the Septuagint. This is likely what Greek-speaking Jews and early Christ-followers used in the synagogues. Because of this, comparing specific words and phrases used in the Septuagint help us better understand an author's word choice in the New Testament. In the Septuagint, translators use *church* (*ekklesia*) over one hundred times to translate the Hebrew word that means "congregation" or "assembly" of the Lord (Numbers 16:3; 20:4; Deuteronomy 23:2-4).[8] The Israelites understood themselves to belong to God because of God's invitation, and God's purposes remain their reason for assembling. Surely, the New Testament writers hear the Septuagint playing in the background as they use this word.

After all, they are a covenantal people. In Old Testament theology in particular, the covenant establishes the relationship between God and God's people.[9] Look at how this shared identity unfolds in these covenants:

- God initiates the covenant through a person, Abraham, with the intent of assembling a people. The Abrahamic covenant (Genesis 12) leads to a people, the Hebrews, who together receive God's blessing in order to be a blessing to the nations.

- In Exodus we read of God remembering the covenant made with the Hebrew people and acting on their behalf (Exodus 2:24).

- God then initiates the Sinai covenants, and as a people they receive the Ten Commandments. The first set of commandments addresses the parameters for God's relationship with them as a people (Exodus 20:1-11). Yet this is only part one. God also cares about their relationships with each other as outlined in the second set of commandments (Exodus 20:12-17).

A shared identity continues throughout the monarchy and the prophets. The people of Israel know they are a covenant people, a people belonging to God. It should be of no surprise then to read this self-perception permeating the New Testament authors' minds as they write to the early Christ-followers. They understand Jesus as the fulfillment of this line of covenants (Mark 14:24) and establish the church (Matthew 16:18; 18:17) based on this shared identity. This vital link remains true for God's people today.

Have you had your cheek swabbed to discover your family's heritage yet? A friend of mine grew up hearing he was Scandinavian with just a bit of Italian. One of his brothers has darker hair than the others so he leaned into this Mediterranean identity. He learned Italian, traveled to Venice and Florence, and now frequently scans Italy's real estate for retirement options. Then, for fun, he sent in a saliva sample. The family is 91 percent Scandinavian—and there is no trace of Italian. Somewhere in their history, the link connecting them to their family's origin—their shared identity—broke. Being Italian is a mere replacement identity. In the same way, Christian identity is always linked to Israel. We too are a covenant people belonging to God. Has the link broken?

Some scholars contend that translating *ekklesia* as "church" is problematic because the word itself does nothing to link Christ-followers with God's relationship with Israel.[10] I have not heard any good proposals for an alternative, but it does compel us to make sure Christians understand the implications of the New Testament word we read translated as "church." Can we even be the family of God without this identity? No. This is why the New Testament authors intend to solidify that the Christ-followers are "Israel reinterpreted and re-understood through the lens of Jesus as Messiah."[11] Severing this link can quickly lead to neglecting our long family history. If we forget our shared identity, the dominant misconception of church as a service provider will reframe our story. We may even adopt a replacement Italian identity like my friend. An autonomous Christian self-perception can overtake our true identity, and subsequently reshape our conceptions, expectations, and practices. Based on my experiences and research, this is already happening.

Enter ministry with young people. If we continue to follow the trajectory of our current history and connect young people to Christ without also linking them to Christ's church, our connection to God's larger work in history will break. Our identity matters. Young people need to know and experience being a people belonging to God. Remember from chapter two that language functions in a social context. Since words live in a dynamic relationship with their environment, we give words meaning. At the same time, the words we use also give meaning to our experiences. This is good news. The words we use in churches and ministries have power. We can choose to use words and phrases that help relink young people to our shared identity. Because the service-provider misconception is so prevalent, even the common ways we speak about the church need to be identity fused. Let's look together at two examples: fellowship and body.

Reinterpreting fellowship: Linked by Christ. *Fellowship* is a familiar word to us. Churches often have *fellowship* halls. We refer to hang out time at youth group as *fellowship*. I remember once color-coding *fellowship* events in blue on the youth ministry calendar. At its core, fellowship refers to gathering around what we share. This can be a common interest like chess or a shared experience such as being a parent. Yet words function in a social environment. When we perceive the church as a service provider, the core meaning of Christian fellowship can devolve into gatherings of the "like-minded" or "*my* small group." Self is the center. By implication, when I am not happy, fellowship must be absent.

There is a center to Christian fellowship—but it is not *me*. Reformed theologian Emil Brunner wrote clarifying statements about the church in a 1953 publication titled *The Misunderstanding of Church*. Brunner wants to avoid the pendulum swing between what he saw as a Catholic collectivist vision of the church (beginning point is the community) and the individualist claims written by Protestant Reformers (beginning point is personal encounter).[12] Brunner claims this doctrine results in a "fundamentally individualistic" conception of the local church and "an external support for faith"—a means to an end.[13] This sounds eerily familiar to our situation when we reduce the church's role to a service provider in support of personal faith. Brunner aims to guard against an individualistic ecclesiology by defining the church as a *fellowship of Christians*.

> The *ekklesia* of the New Testament, the fellowship of Christian believers, is precisely not that which every "church" is at least in part—an institution, a something. The body of Christ is nothing other than a fellowship of persons. It is the "fellowship of Christ" (1 Corinthians 1:9) or "fellowship of the Holy Spirit" (2 Corinthians 13:14; Philippians 2:1), where fellowship or *koinonia* signifies a common participation, a togetherness, a community life. The faithful are bound to each other through their common sharing in Christ and in the Holy Spirit, but what they have in common is precisely no "thing," no "it," but a "he," Christ and His Holy Spirit.[14]

For Brunner the basis of Christian fellowship extends far beyond our experiences and momentary feelings of togetherness. Christian community is more than our shared commitment to Christ or supportive companionship on a long journey. Fellowship in Christ is our identity. What binds us together always comes from outside and beyond us because it is not us who create or make this bond. Christ through the Spirit *holds* us in fellowship with each other. We are linked by Christ.

Even though it may be overused, I still love the knot game. Everyone stands in a circle and reaches across to grab the hands of two different people. The result is a human knot that may try your patience. The group needs to figure out how to untie the knot by climbing over joined hands, crawling under arms, and twisting around each other. All the while, the linked hands must never let go.

So it is with Christian fellowship. Christ links our hands in fellowship through the Spirit. We cannot create, produce, or even consume this fellowship. As Brunner says, there is no "it" in fellowship. Only Christ. Christ is the active, linking center of Christian fellowship. Because this fellowship does not depend on me (or us), we live by hope. Christian togetherness fails all the time. Yet our hope remains in the one linking our hands and lives together. Dietrich Bonhoeffer captures this, saying, "A Christian comes to others only through Jesus Christ."[15] Although this may sound abstract, Bonhoeffer speaks practically here. Our relationships should express that we are linked by Christ. How do young people experience this linkedness in your church, and how might you build on these experiences?

Reinterpreting body: Who we are. "Have you heard what happened?" Elisabeth, a sixth grader, almost knocks me over in her excitement. "Meghan Trainor refuses to be photoshopped in pictures and videos because they are 'not her.'" Through all the chatter surrounding this newsflash, Meghan Trainor, a popular singer-songwriter, is making a profound statement about the human body. Elisabeth, even if for a moment, hears Meghan connect her physical body to her identity. In a photoshopping culture, this is an insight we need to hear as individuals, but what does this tell us about the church?

As New Testament scholar Luke Timothy Johnson explains, there are different cultural understandings of the body.[16] Contemporary philosophical frameworks, scientific discoveries, and technological advances shape our working definition of the body in Western societies. We predominantly think of the body as a possession or property. I can say, "I have a body." It is something I possess, own, can sell, and have rights over. There are both positive and negative implications of this conception. Since my essence is not bound to my body, I can check the "organ donor" box on my license without losing myself. Yet, alarmingly, viewing the body this way can also turn the body into a sexual and material object to be owned or bought by others. Even if there are some positive implications, Meghan Trainor reminds us that there are dangerous implications when we reduce the body.

Johnson argues that in Paul's culture the body is understood as *who I am* rather than *what I have*. We cannot be absent from our bodies. Rather, we have bodily experiences: moving, thinking, feeling, doing. Johnson declares, "I cannot detach myself from my body as though it were not me."[17] A body also lives in a physical environment where we eat, get sick, act, and die. We experience others through our body's senses, which means our bodies are also socially oriented. When Paul calls the church the body of Christ, he speaks out of this understanding. Johnson concludes that Paul's definition of body leaves no room for a radical individualism in the faith community. Like a body, the church is *who we are*, not *what we have*. Our shared identity is screaming for attention when we hear this phrase. We don't give young people the church as something to possess or even reject—these young people *are* the church.

The relationship between a Christian and the church is vital. The church is not a building, an organization, or, now adding to the list, a service provider. The church is the people. Church is not where we go (building) or what we join (organization). We do not have a church (possession) or choose a church (product). The church is who we are. To say the church is a people belonging to God is to affirm our shared identity forever linked with God's covenant people we read about in the Old Testament. We are a fellowship

> We don't give young people the church as something to possess or even reject—these young people *are* the church.

held together by Christ, and we are a body. Teaching and embodying this understanding for young people has tremendous implications for our life together and vision that should be the beginning point of all ministry with young people. Knowing this vital identity also leads us to ask about the purpose of our relationships.

A VITAL PURPOSE

CHRIST IS RECONCILING RELATIONSHIPS

MEET SYDNEY WHEN SHE IS A SEVENTH GRADER. She comes to everything. Sydney is what I like to call a soaker because she wants to take in everything she can to help her grow in her faith. It seems like every time I get on the bus at the end of a trip, Sydney saves a seat for me. She likes to ask questions and try out her own answers. Our relationship feels free. We can challenge each other's ideas and benefit from the debate. At times, we know we are onto something and share a fist-bump celebration. Fast-forward ten years, and the tone of our conversation is very different. Sydney challenges many beliefs she held as a teenager. In no way does she reject her faith; she is a steadfast Christ-follower. However, our common ground is shrinking. Sydney and I sit in different theological camps. Our conversations are now tense and often accusing. I grieve the loss of this relationship even as I find myself avoiding her.

In chapter three I argue that our shared identity is vital because we are a people belonging to God. It would be nice if this vision was like the perfect family photo captured when everyone is smiling. Yet in real life we rarely get this shot. Instead, reality breaks in when I recognize that I am writing about my strained relationship with Sydney. You see, our shared identity raises a question: *What is God's intention for relationships among Christ-followers?* I am not talking about God's overall purposes, yet surely what follows includes these. Neither am I describing the multiple purposes of the church, even if this is one of the purposes. I am focusing on the relationship between individual Christians with a shared identity. What is God's purpose for this relationship? What does God intend for Sydney and me?

Dietrich Bonhoeffer's theology of sociality guides us toward an answer. Like me, he wants to avoid the pendulum swing that focuses only on the person *or* only the community. He is aware of this tendency among his contemporaries. On one side, he is reading philosophers who describe the human person by emphasizing the individual. On the other side, he hears the social scientists emphasize the community by describing how the social environment forms the person. Bonhoeffer expresses dissatisfaction with both approaches because he finds that neither the isolated individual nor the socially formed person to be adequate for Christian theology. His 1927 doctoral dissertation, *Sanctorum Communio*, is his response to this dilemma and explains why simultaneously recognizing the person and the community is critical for the Christian faith.

Bonhoeffer builds a definition of the church by identifying three states of existence: the primal, the sinful, and the *sanctorum communio* (the local church). Think of each state as the solid, liquid, and gas form of water. Even though the molecular formula for water always includes oxygen and hydrogen, the relationship among the water molecules is distinct in each state. With ice, the relationship is tight-knit and still. With liquid and steam, the relationship involves increasing distance and movement. Similarly, Bonhoeffer explains three distinct states that include the same three participants—God, the person, and others—but the relationship among them changes. He does this to compare and contrast the different relationship dynamics in each community.

PRIMAL STATE: THE ULTIMATE COMMUNITY

We are in a planning meeting for the upcoming year. Becca bursts in with four event ideas, and George has a mission project in the works. I invite everyone to call out ideas, and we write them on the board. I then ask everyone to pause. Becca and George both give me half smiles and a friendly eye roll. They know me. Before I can make plans, I need to know where we are heading. Once we set next year's goals based on our larger vision, we can revisit the list to make a concrete plan. Becca and George are familiar with my resistance to plans without purpose. I am a big-picture thinker. (As you might guess, I need detail people in the room to make sure things get done.) I suspect this is why I find Bonhoeffer's primal community a good starting place—because it captures the big picture.

The word *primal* can be misleading. It does not mean first, which would lead us to believe Bonhoeffer is talking about Genesis 1–2 and the first community. Instead, *primal* means ultimate. The primal state is an eschatological (in the end) big picture. Ultimately, what is God doing? God is reconciling all things, and this reconciliation includes our individual relationships with God as well as our relationships with one another.

The ultimate community is made up of people with differing wills. Isn't that odd? If this is God's purpose, wouldn't unity be a more plausible focus than difference? For Bonhoeffer, having a will is central to being human because it demonstrates a person's activity or agency. This is no mere philosophical idea; rather, will is a concrete experience. I demonstrate my will by expressing an idea or having expectations, desires, and opinions of someone else. This establishes me as an independent person. Without will, humans would be robotic or absorbed into the sameness of others. *Without will, I would cease to be a person distinguishable from the community.* Differing wills exist every time two people meet. Therefore, to be in relationship is always to encounter difference.

In Bonhoeffer's ultimate community, Sydney and I retain our independent wills, yet our relationship is characterized by *mutual love and service*.[1] We are free to follow God's

To be in relationship is always to encounter difference.

demonstration of love to us: Christ humbles himself by entering human flesh, washing the disciples' feet, and walking the road to Golgotha. In Bonhoeffer's words, "The miracle of the Christian concept of community is that love for God involves submission, but that God's love, in ruling, serves."[2] God's love comes alive in relationships as Christ empowers persons with distinct wills to serve each other. I am not forced to worship God, love Sydney, or serve others. Experiencing God's transforming love awakens my will, and I can freely love and serve. This is the ultimate community: reciprocal relationships expressing love through service. As Bonhoeffer claims, "Agreement without this reciprocal attitude is merely parallel existence."[3] In the primal state, Sydney and I are living in reconciled relationship with God and each other. Remember that this community is not like putting your car into reverse and driving backward to the pre-fall garden where sin's consequences are not known. Instead, each person knows sin and the destructive divide that results. Because there is such a contrast, our encounter with God's transforming love is rich and colorful.

Miroslav Volf's description of the last judgment amplifies what this experience might be like. Since Christ stands for us as judge and pronounces "no condemnation" (Romans 8:1), reconciliation of all things is possible. But what might this experience be like? For Volf there is a difference between reconciliation as a "fresh start" and a "social affair."[4] Fresh start reconciliation is like the person who spills ink all over a page and then receives a clean piece of paper to start over. Yet a fresh start wipes away the experience of spilling the ink and being cleaned up. If this were the final reconciliation, we would not actually *experience* being reconciled. Instead, Volf imagines reconciliation to be more like a social event. When we fully encounter God's grace-filled love and forgiveness, we gain through Christ the capacity to forgive and reconcile with one another. This is the redemption of *all* that is broken, hurt, and estranged. Try to wrap your head around the idea that this includes all people across time and space. We will experience God's transforming love redeeming "yesterday, today, and tomorrow—redemption of our whole lived life."[5]

It's easy to imagine this scene when it includes reconciling with those we love. The 1999 Mercy Me song "I Can Only Imagine" captures this well. The songwriter writes this song in response to the pain of losing a loved one. The music video portrays people looking through empty frames, hurt and confused over such weighty loss. As the lyrics progress, a vision of standing in God's presence with God's glory shines through and fills the empty frames with faces—beloved fathers, daughters, spouses, and friends. I long for that day, don't you? Yet Volf reminds us that reconciliation also includes embracing our enemies. He states, "Reconciliation will take place only when former enemies have moved toward each other and embraced each other as belonging to the same communion of love."[6] In addition to pictures of loved ones, faces of enemies will fill the frames. *Enemy* is a strong word, yet it gets to the heart of the matter. God's love will bring about a reconciliation party, one in which we experience and actively participate. What a day!

I suspect this is what Bonhoeffer envisions when he describes the primal state. He proposes far more than an abstract vision of an ideal world because, for him, theology matters only as it influences how we live. In the ultimate community, families, friends, and, yes, enemies all experience being reconciled in relationship with God and one another. This then becomes woven into the fabric of our new life together. My contentious friendship with Sydney is but one example of the current inflamed discord between Christians. "I can only imagine" a reconciliation party where we stand in awe before God and people (the *us* versus *them* camps) and are freed by God's grace and mercy to apologize, listen, forgive, understand, and heal. Because we are immersed in God's transforming love, we experience redeemed relationships marked by willful love and service. Bonhoeffer's ultimate community is our deep hope and longing, isn't it? This is the big picture where we are heading.

However, there is another state.

SINFUL STATE: NO COMMUNITY

The sinful state can be summed up in two words: *broken relationships*. Sydney and I have a broken relationship. Disagreeing consumes us, and we struggle to serve each other. It feels impossible to express love for each other with a wall of tension and disappointment between us. And this is a mild example, is it not? Sin causes deep pain and hurt that can influence the rest of our lives. Just as sin breaks our relationship with God, sin's effects wreak havoc on our relationships with each other.

It is more common for theologians and pastors to define the nature or character of sin, such as missing the mark, a transgression, or an iniquity. Bonhoeffer takes a different approach. Sin *is* its consequences on relationships. Sin severs our relationships with God and others. Why? In Bonhoeffer's words, "The fall replaced love with selfishness. This gave rise to the break in immediate community with God, and likewise in human community."[7] Even Bonhoeffer's description of sin's guilt is more than a psychological or spiritual state. Sin is the concrete experience of a broken relationship.[8] Contrast the sinful state with ultimate community. Mutual love mutates into self-absorption. Service dissolves into self-centeredness. Relationships shift from giving to demanding. People act in self-interest with unashamed indifference for others. In the sinful state the person's self-focused will results in isolation and loneliness. Sydney and I drift away from each other, and the gap between us fills with anger and pain. This is life with an estranged relationship with God, and we find ourselves alienated from other people.

Like Ebenezer Scrooge on Christmas Eve, there is no community. The Ghost of Christmas Yet to Come leads Scrooge through scenes where person after person finds relief in a nameless man's death. Greed marks the unidentified man's life, and people express being better off without him. Scrooge begs the silent, hooded ghost to tell him the identity of this man. The answer comes in a neglected graveyard where Scrooge finds his own name scrolled on the stone. Scrooge responds in horror, "No, Spirit! Oh no, no!" His greed results in unbearable isolation.[9]

Ralph experiences life without community in William Golding's *Lord of the Flies*. A war is underway, and a plane full of evacuating British schoolboys crashes, unseen, on a tropical island. Ralph quickly assumes leadership. He knows they need the fire's constant smoke to signal for help. At first, all the boys follow his lead. They figure out how to hunt for food and create shelter. But eventually they become distracted, and their desire to play leads to deep division. Rallying around the need to send a smoke signal dissolves, and savagery ensues. They challenge Ralph's authority, and he flees for safety after becoming the young hunters' target.

> He knelt among the shadows and felt his isolation bitterly. They were savages it was true; but they were human, and the ambushing fears of the deep night were coming on.
>
> Ralph moaned faintly. Tired though he was, he could not relax and fall into a well of sleep for fear of the tribe. Might it not be possible to walk boldly into the fort, say—"I've got [peace]," laugh lightly and sleep among the others? Pretend they were still boys, schoolboys who had said, "Sir, yes, Sir"—and worn caps? Daylight might have answered yes; but darkness and the horrors of death said no. Lying there in the darkness, he knew he was an outcast.[10]

Medieval poet Dante graphically describes sin's consequences in the *Divine Comedy*. The poet Virgil takes Dante on a journey through hell's gate bearing the inscription, "Abandon all hope, ye who enter here."[11] They walk through nine winding circles that lead downward to the place that holds Satan. Each circle represents people suffering the consequences of a specific sin such as greed, gluttony, and lust. The severity of sin increases the closer Virgil and Dante get to Satan. I am struck by the final circle—treachery. People who betray special relationships fill this place. Dante vividly describes people stuck in a frozen lake because their actions remove them from the warmth of God's love. Because they reject human bonds, they remain in frozen isolation—except for two bodies frozen together as one gnaws on the other. "I saw two frozen in one hole so closely, that the one head was a cap to the other; and as bread is chewed for hunger, so the uppermost put his teeth into the other there where the brain joins with the nape."[12]

What a graphic depiction of the sinful state. Without intervention, our differing wills dissolve into self-absorption and "eating" those closest to us.

Literature captures what is all too familiar in our lives. Sin alienates and isolates. The child who suffers from neglect does not find love. Playground bullying crushes youthful hope. Parents perpetuate unhealthy family dynamics generation after generation. Church leaders wield power irresponsibly. Adults marginalize kids with physical and mental challenges. Sydney and I create the wall between us. In the sinful state, we do not experience community because "everyone lives their own life, rather than all living the same life in God."[13] We are stuck in a frozen lake.

The contrast between the primal and the sinful states is stark. Yet we are not left alone. Christ comes from the outside—because salvation cannot come from our own efforts—to reconcile our relationships with God *and* one another. We are free to repent of greed and come out of hiding. The result is the third state—the *sanctorum communio*.

SANCTORUM COMMUNIO: RECIPROCAL COMMUNITY

By acting in history through Christ, God reconciles the disparity between the primal and sinful states. Christ does for us what we cannot do for ourselves and melts the frozen lake of our self-created isolation. This is familiar to us. We know there is nothing we can do to earn our salvation, for "while we were still sinners, Christ died for us" (Romans 5:8). God acts in Christ so every person might be reconciled to God. In Christ, salvation's pathway breaks open.

But this is not all Christ does. Like setting a route on Google maps, Christ's self-giving life, death, and resurrection establishes our trajectory toward the ultimate community where we express love for God in service to one another. Christ does not simply come once and for all but continues to act on our behalf by coming to us again and again. Bonhoeffer uses the German word *Stellvertretung* to describe Christ's present redeeming activity. As theologian Clifford Green explains, "*Stellvertretung* is one of Bonhoeffer's fundamental theological concepts throughout his writings. Literally, it means to represent in place of another—to act, advocate, intercede on behalf of another."[14] In the reciprocal community, Christ's activity reconciles us to God *and* opens the way for us to make peace with one another. Christ enters the gap we cannot fill. Sydney and I are not left to eat each other in the frozen lake of our differing wills. Our hearts melt, and our wills are free to act in loving ways.

Even though this often feels light-years away from the ultimate community, the reciprocal community comes into existence in real time. Bonhoeffer proclaims, "In Christ God loves human beings and opens the divine heart; and in giving God's own self to sinful human beings God renews them at the same time and thus makes the new community possible and real; but this means that *God's love wills community.*"[15] What does willing community look like? For Bonhoeffer, this means people who are "with-each-other" become people who are "for-each-other."

I am late for church, and people are already on their feet singing with the worship team. As I walk quickly down the aisle toward an open seat, I catch a glimpse of Rory right next to the open chair. I freeze. Has she seen me? No. Good. I creep backwards, head to the other side of the room, and add my voice to those praising God. On this day, I am barely willing to be-with-Rory and certainly not willing to be-for-Rory.

At a search committee meeting earlier in the week, Rory refuses to listen to me. She wants to hire a candidate for the church's open ministry position. When I scan the résumé, I discover it is full of inconsistencies and clearly inaccurate information. I make a call and discover that he never held a ministry position as listed on his resumé. Clearly, honesty is not a dominant character trait. Rory ignores my concerns and pushes the committee to affirm the applicant. As far as I am concerned, Rory can stay on her side of the church, and I will stay on mine. We are *with* each other in a frozen lake.

In Ephesians 2, Paul reminds the Gentiles that once they were "excluded from citizenship in Israel and foreigners to the covenants" (v. 12). But now because of Christ, the Gentiles are "fellow citizens" and "members of God's household" (v. 19). Notice what Christ's reconciling work does in the passage. He destroys the barrier, "the dividing wall of hostility" (v. 14), between Jew and Gentile. We know that this barrier was both religious and cultural. But surely it was also a wall built from generations worth of discord, stereotypes, and plain dislike. Christ is their "peace" and "has made the two groups one" (v. 14). The Jews and Gentiles are now "being built together to become a dwelling in which God lives by his Spirit" (v. 22). This means redemption has social implications for Christian community. Breaking down the dividing wall is not only for a celestial city or other-worldly eternal destination. Jews and Gentiles were to stand together in Christ in real time. With hope, they press through the painful wall of bricks, as the Spirit works to "put to death their hostility" (v. 16). This is true for us too. Christ comes to free us from the frozen lake filled with our relationships with our Christian brothers and sisters. When we are in hiding for being ousted by the community, Christ is actively doing for us what we cannot do for ourselves. Christ makes living at peace with each other a possibility.

Bonhoeffer is not naive. Even though he defines these three communities before the rise of the Third Reich in Germany, he understands the church is often a *hot mess*. Fully eradicating sin and its consequences on our relationships with others will not occur until Christ returns. The final reconciliation party awaits the ultimate community. The *sanctorum communio* is therefore an act of faith as we trust in Christ's *present* activity to advocate and intercede.

It is as if we are all a bunch of positively charged hydrogen atoms. Since we need to bond with negatively charged atoms, our differing wills act like positive charges that repel one another. We struggle to bond on our own. Christ resembles a negatively charged oxygen atom pulling hydrogen atoms toward him to form a water molecule and making it possible for us also to then bond with one another. When enough of these bonds form, a cohesive body of water emerges—the body of Christ.

What is the purpose of the relationship between the Christian and the church? Why do young people need to bond with the body of Christ? They need to experience Christ's reconciling activity here and now. We live at a time when young people use experience as the test for what is true. If they encounter a church filled with people who sit beside each other chattering about unity without actually prioritizing reconciliation, young people see a loose institution of untransformed people. Our churches simply lose credibility when what we claim about Christ's redemption does not influence our relationships with one another. We are already painfully aware of the response—young people leave.

The good news is that right now Christ is able to do for us what we are unable to do ourselves. It is not enough for me to be-with-Rory and to be-with-Sydney. It is in Christian community where Christ's self-giving love enables us to be *for-one-another*. Our churches and ministries need to align with the trajectory of the ultimate community. We are *en route*. This will mean prioritizing be-coming a people of God where

> **Our churches simply lose credibility when what we claim about Christ's redemption does not influence our relationships with one another.**

love—yes, amid our differing hydrogen wills—marks our communities. Christ who "preached peace" (Ephesians 2:17) creates peace. Molecules form, bonds between them grow, and the body emerges. Christ's self-giving love reconciles us to God, melts the frozen lake, calls us out of hiding, and enables us to love and serve one another. Young people need to hear *and see* this good news. This is the heartbeat of a reciprocal church.

A VITAL AVENUE

THE SPIRIT TRANSFORMS YOU, ME, AND US

WE ARE ON A YOUTH RETREAT during my junior year of high school when I make what feels like a life-altering discovery. My youth leader explains the importance of having a daily "quiet time with God." It is like a master key opening the path toward Christian maturity. I walk away hearing that Christian discipleship depends on my ability to read the Bible on my own and develop an active prayer life. The more time I spend alone with God, the more fruit I will see in my life.

I confess to being an overachiever. It would surely be better for me to work this out in counseling instead of embedding this impulse in my growing theological framework. Even so, discovering the "master key" to attaining Christian maturity at age seventeen is appealing to me (and often celebrated by others). I memorize Scripture. I pray Scripture. I post Scripture on my bathroom mirror. I fill notebooks with prayers, wake up early to pray, light candles, and discover the prompting power of music. The key does unlock deep communion with God. It also shapes my reputation at school as I share my experiences. People know I am a *really* strong Christian. Youth leaders applaud my growth and reward me with leadership positions reserved for the spiritually mature kids. The master key appears to have worked.

Curiously, there is another side of my life. In my hand, I hold a list of soured friendships. Jean and I have been best friends since middle school. Back then, we tell each other everything, dress the same, think the same, and truly enjoy being together. By high school, we have our own unique interests, but our friendship remains strong. Then Jean decides to run for senior class president. So do I. At first we laugh about the friendly competition. But I am an overachiever. Losing is not an option. I pull together a group of friends to help me run a big campaign and write an unforgettable speech. I have this. Votes are tallied, and there is a tie between Jean and Arthur. I am out. My Christian maturity should shine in this moment. But it does not. Pride and jealousy pour out as I join Arthur's campaign for the runoff vote and see to it that Jean is defeated. We never speak again.

I incorrectly understood Christian maturity as perfecting the quiet time. Frankly, there was more at play in my error than my over-achieving self. The gospel package I was hearing had little to say about my friendships, a Christian's shared identity, or God's intention to reconcile relationships. Maturity simply meant me knowing Jesus. I did learn about the importance of modeling Christ to others. Yet the reason behind this was to support other people's relationship with God rather than emphasize reconciling relationships as core to the gospel. Solitary disciplines do foster personal communion with God, which are essential for Christian maturity. However, once again we find only the partial vision. The service-provider paradigm relegates relationships to the realm of personal spiritual development. Me and my growth is the end, and the relationship is the means. We need a fuller vision. God also intends to reconcile relationships, moving us from the sinful community into the reciprocal community as we anticipate God's ultimate community where people live in reconciled relationship with God and others. Just as I commit to enriching my communion with God, I am also called to work out my friendship with Jean. This leads us to an important question: What is the avenue for fostering this type of maturing faith?

I have a pretty straightforward answer: relationships. Our relationships with others, and Christians in particular, are an avenue for God's redemptive work in our midst. A Christian's relationship with the church is vital because relationships are a means of grace. To grasp how vast this paradigm shift will be, let's examine how this partial vision of the Christian faith creeps into the way we interpret the Scriptures.

I incorrectly understood Christian maturity as perfecting the quiet time.

TRAINING OUR INTERPRETIVE LENS

"You should spend more time with young people." Is the *you* in this sentence singular or plural? Yep, this is a trick question. Welcome to the English language. As you learned in elementary school, context is the only way to know if *you* is singular or plural. (Texans reading this should start a petition to make *y'all* the official plural *you* and end the confusion.) *You* is obviously all over the pages of the Bible. Yet there is no singular-plural confusion here because both Hebrew and Greek specify *you* as singular or plural. Translations can generally make this clear in our Bibles, but we still have to read the context to interpret accurately. In reality, there is more at play when we come across *you* in the biblical text.

Just like we live in a different historical and cultural context than the biblical authors, we also live in a different social world. The social world includes social dynamics among people who are part of larger social systems.[1] Words, behaviors, and values hold meanings that are always part of a social context. Learning about the biblical author's social world will enrich our understanding of the text as well as help us avoid interpreting the Bible based on our own social world.

People in the United States and much of the Western world pre-dominantly live in a social context marked by an individualistic ori-entation.[2] This means we put the individual before the community. We measure success based on personal achievements. Rather than prioritizing a community's values or heritage, we focus on developing a person's ability with an eye toward the future. This emphasis is clear even in the terms used by psychologists to define aspects of maturity such as *individuation* (Carl Jung) and *independence* (Erik Erikson). Both concepts highlight separating from others. Maturity in an indi-vidualistic social world generally means gaining the capacity to stand on your own two feet and achieving personal success.

The title of the 2006 movie *Failure to Launch* starring Matthew McConaughey and Sarah Jessica Parker captures this well. Like many of his friends, McConaughey's character is in his thirties, holds a full-time job, and *could* move out on his own. Instead, he enjoys the comforts of living in his parents' house. He has not fully launched into adulthood, which is perceived as a failure at his age. His parents want to give him a final push out of the nest, so they hire an "expert"—enter Sarah Jessica Parker. She promises that once she begins a relationship with him that his confidence will build, and he will be able to detach from his parents. Separation marks maturity, and not launching out on one's own is a failure.

In an individualist social world, successful parenting is helping our kids find their place in the world. Gaining independence from the family is a mark of adulthood. Individual skills and abilities that prepare for the future are primary. Growing up means learning who I am as I separate and become independent. We carry this into our interpretation of faith as well. We want young people to take on faith "as your own" and feel concerned for those who still have their "parents' faith."

The social world of ancient Near East cultures is significantly dif-ferent. They have a collectivist orientation and a group-oriented per-sonality. People see themselves as inextricably connected to others. In fact, the community provides identity. Rather than launching into independence, what matters is belonging and contributing to the group. Focusing on the future means preserving the traditions and values of the group. In a collectivist social world, a person wants to act in ways that bring honor to the community and avoid bringing shame upon the community. A version of the following story landed in my newsfeed on Facebook, and it captures the distinctiveness of a group-oriented personality. After doing a little research on its origin, I discovered that people use this story to teach the *Ubuntu* principle, a traditional value in some South African collectivist cultures.

A cultural anthropologist conducts an experiment with African children. They tell the children there is a large basket of treats hidden nearby. The rules are simple: whoever finds the basket gets to enjoy all the treats. Excited children run in all directions hunting for the basket. Curiously, they do not go alone but in twos and threes, holding hands as they search. One group quickly finds the basket and squeals in delight, calling the other children together. They form a circle, sit down, and place the basket in the middle. The cultural anthropologist reminds the winners of the rules. The treats belong to the one who finds the basket. Confused, the children look at each other and ask, How can one of us enjoy the treats if the others have none? In a collectivist social world, one person's experience depends on another's, while an individualist social world values individual success.

I am describing differences between two social worlds rather than evaluating them. Both the collectivist and individualistic orientations have inherent strengths and pose particular challenges. The former might disregard the person, and the latter can neglect the community. In the end the orientations of these two views have distinct expectations and values: achievement is what we do versus what I do, relationships benefit the community versus the person, and *faith is ours versus mine.*

Back to grammar. Because Westerners live in a predominantly individualist social world and use the same word *you* for the singular and plural, singular *you* will become the default interpretation even if the context is clearly plural *you*. This affects how we interpret the Bible. It is as if we are wearing glasses that alter the contours of meaning. We use an individualistic lens without even knowing it. We especially default to this lens when reading the Epistles because the material directly relates to our lives. Instead, we need to train our interpretive eyes and look through a collectivist lens like the original readers would have. We will then discover that these letters describe the relationships among Christians as a unique avenue for a maturing Christian faith.

PLURAL YOU (OR Y'ALL) IN COLOSSIANS 3:1-17

As an example, let's look at the letter to churches in Colossae. There appears to be some kind of false teaching swirling through the community. Scholars propose numerous possibilities, but the exact false teaching is not clear in the letter.[3] However, the author's focus on God's reconciling work in Christ is clear. The letter begins with a hymn declaring who Christ is, and this sets the stage for the rest of the letter (Colossians 1:15-20). Christ is creator, sustainer, and reconciler of all things. The author wants the Christ-followers in Colossae to feel confident that they are not in need of anything that these false teachings offer. God's reconciling activity in Christ is sufficient for them. They belong to Christ, "having been buried with him in baptism, in which you were also raised with him through your faith in the working of God, who raised him from the dead" (Colossians 2:12). There are also implications for those who died with Christ, for the old way of doing things also died with Christ.

A noteworthy shift occurs between Colossians 2 and 3. Up to this point, the author has been emphasizing how through their baptism, they join Christ who died and was raised (Colossians 2:11-13). Yet in Colossians 3:1, the author drops "died" and retains "raised," turning the reader's attention toward life right now: "Since, then, you have been *raised* with Christ, set your hearts on things above." These Christ-followers are presently being raised, and Christ establishes a new way for them to be together. They are called to participate in a new social world.[4] These Christ-followers are to take off or "put to death" (Colossians 3:5) what belongs to the old order and put on or "clothe" themselves like the new order (v. 12).

You (including your, yourself, etc.) in this passage is plural. If you pay careful attention to this in the English translation, the context makes this clear. However, our individualistic orientation is powerful, and the default singular *you* takes hold. It acts like a pair of glasses shaping our interpretation of the text. Compare the singular *you* and plural *you* interpretations of Colossians 3:1-4 in the following paragraphs. I only have to drop an "s" from two nouns to make the context a singular *you*.

Read every *you* as singular:

> Since, then, *you* have been raised with Christ, set *your* hearts on things above, where Christ is, seated at the right hand of God. Set *your* minds on things above, not on earthly things. For *you* died, and *your* life is now hidden with Christ in God. When Christ, who is *your* life, appears, then *you* also will appear with him in glory.

For emphasis (and fun), I have included *y'all* and *y'all's* when *you* is plural:

> Since, then, *y'all* have been raised with Christ, set *y'all's* hearts on things above, where Christ is, seated at the right hand of God. Set *y'all's* minds on things above, not on earthly things. For *y'all* died, and *y'all's* life is now hidden with Christ in God. When Christ, who is *y'all's* life, appears, then *y'all* also will appear with him in glory.

Quite the difference. The singular interpretation describes an enclosed, private relationship with God. And it sounds very familiar, doesn't it? This is the minimized gospel package. Being raised with Christ morphs into a call for only personal discipleship. If we continue to read the passage through the singular *you* lens—so familiar to those of us who live in an individualistic social world—we find a list of vices to remove and virtues to put on. The passage becomes a call for personal piety. It is the master key to Christian maturity all over again. I have died, and I am being raised with Christ.

But this is not what the passage says. *You* is plural. Christ is our life, and we will appear with him in glory. We have died, and we are to be raised with Christ. The list of vices and virtues only accentuates the communal aspect of our raisedness (Colossians 3:5-17). There are two sets of vices.[5] The first set includes sins of self-centeredness: sexual immorality, impurity, lust, evil desires, and greed. Sins of speech comprise the second set: anger, wrath, malice, slander, and filthy language. One vice stands alone—do not lie. None of these vices are solo acts. Greed, slander, and lying all require speaking to or about another. Why does this matter? Because being raised with Christ has implications for our relationships with one another. The vices undermine the community's peace and unity. The vices not only will ruin individual lives; they also destroy community.

In the same way, all the virtues listed in the passage involve other people. They all define behaviors that enhance community. Compassion and kindness direct our way of relating to others. Humility suggests a posture of service and self-sacrifice to others. Gentleness and patience require bearing with each other's vices. Forgiveness means there is someone who needs to be forgiven. Much like Bonhoeffer's emphasis on mutual love and service, the pinnacle virtue that "binds them all together" is love *for others* (v. 14). This is not a love for self or even love for God. Setting their "hearts on things above" where they one day will be raised *together* with Christ has implications now. Transforming relationships is a sign of being raised in Christ. In addition, remember the theme of the letter. The author is reminding these Christ-followers that they need nothing other than God's reconciling activity in Christ. Christ through the Spirit continues to transform persons and communities. To be raised with Christ is to "put on" community-building behaviors. Just like we work hard to commune with God on our own, we are also called to deepen our communion with one another.

At this point, it is appropriate to wonder if this vision of community transformation exists only because it was written out of and for a collectivist social world. Meaning, if it were written in an individualistic social world would the message remain? The answer is straightforward. We interpret the implications of a passage not only based on the passage itself but also according to the larger biblical narrative. What is God's purpose for the relationships between and among Christians? Christ works to reconcile us to God and to one another. Colossians 3 is a practical description of the gospel's implications. We just need to be aware of the interpretive glasses we are wearing.

To be raised with Christ is to "put on" community-building behaviors.

AVENUE OF GRACE

To be raised in Christ includes participating in a community where our behavior transforms from community *destroying* to community *building*. Our relationships with other Christians are an avenue for learning to be patient, gentle, and forgiving. In the process, I am transformed, you are transformed, and we—a people belonging to God—are transformed.

We are on the worst trip ever. It is spring break, and we drive two vans full of kids from Tennessee to the Florida swamplands to spend the week in a hospital for severely disabled adults. Everything on the trip seems to go wrong. We take a wrong turn that adds hours to the drive. In a parking lot, I back into a tall metal pole with the church van. The air is hot and sticky, and the rain falls endlessly. The camp where we spend our nights is primitive and not well-kept. Clearly, the spiders believe they have squatters' rights. On top of this, none of us are prepared for the flood of intense emotions accompanying our time at the medical facility. Seeing human beings with such physical and mental challenges overwhelms us. The building is old, hot, and full of strong odors. The staff is extremely dedicated, but they need more resources to care for these people.

It is day three, and the conflicts in our group begin among kids and leaders alike. None of us have the capacity to respond well to one another. Each night we cram into a hot room at the camp. I am supposed to lead this devotional time but have nothing to offer. I read passages of Scripture and pray feeble prayers with nothing to say.

The kids sense the Spirit first. Girls demonstrate humility as they take turns sleeping on the floor. Compassion marks the way the boys care for people at the home. I watch as even those who want to escape our new friends' suffering instead choose generosity and kindness. Patience comes while waiting for showers. Since the kids are a step ahead of the leaders, we disappoint them. Their efforts to forgive us inspire me to seek to be forgiven. These are not the kind of things you learn during a quiet time or listening to worship music. The difficult circumstances exasperate our differing wills and surprisingly become an avenue for the Spirit's transformation. This is the reciprocal church. Christ's activity among us is evident as some of our vices transform into virtues. Years later, this trip still stands out as one of the most important experiences in each of our lives.

Relationships are an avenue for the Spirit's activity. It took ten years of marriage to resist my stubbornness and be the first to apologize. Working with me will surely require my colleagues to learn patience. Practicing humility begins only when our wills collide. Solitary disciplines of the faith, as crucial as they are, do not teach such things. Our brokenness and difficulties with one another reveal our inabilities. We come to the end of ourselves as we are. Here we encounter Christ, who, by the Spirit, does for us what we cannot do for ourselves, and there is hope for us personally as our relationships begin to transform. But how? This transformation sounds good but how does it actually occur?

VITAL SOURCE

After the birth of our second child, I become very ill. I spend over two weeks in the hospital and receive multiple blood transfusions along with a long list of drugs. The doctors contemplate my unusual case and hope for better results. This is a desperate time for me. Stories of people in distress dance through my head. I remember how their cries for help are met with deep and powerful encounters with God's presence. But not so for me. I feel God's absence. As much as I call out to God, the silence is deafening.

Following a life-saving surgery, my husband pushes my wheelchair to the car as we finally leave the hospital after twenty-one days. I am still weak, and my energy is spent once I reach the couch at home. My tired gaze rests on the carpet. Without thinking I say to my husband, "How come the floor hasn't been vacuumed?" Geoff's facial expression changes like a chameleon's colors: from anger to confusion to under-standing. He says quietly, "Sharon, do you know what's been going on here?" He begins unfolding the events from my family's perspective: I am not in the hospital long before my mom decides I should not be alone. I am just too sick. My mom, my dad, and my husband take turns rotating through care of our children and care of me, 24/7. Geoff is working on top of this. He comes while I cry each morning. My mom and I talk in between tests each afternoon. My dad lies by my bed every night when I am the sickest. Pastors come to visit me, and family and friends provide meals at home. Clearly, there is no time to vacuum the carpet.

You see, God did answer my cries for help by surrounding our family, and particularly me, with the tangible presence of love from our community. Yet, at the time, I missed it. I missed it because I was looking for God's presence in some sort of private, mystical encounter. Moses did not make the same mistake.

God's presence: A conditional identity. Backstory: Moses is deeply troubled. While he is on the mountain receiving tabernacle-building instructions from Yahweh, the people waiting below are overcome by doubt and fear. They seek security in the lesser, yet more familiar, gods of Egypt. With Aaron's help, they mold the infamous golden calf. When Moses discovers them, he is surely overwhelmed with emotions ranging from anger to grief to distress. However, these feelings only accompany his greater fear—*the loss of God's presence.*

Figuring out how to host God's presence is a dominant theme in Exodus, according to Old Testament scholar Walter Brueggemann. Since God is not "casually or easily available to Israel," this is an ongoing challenge.[6] Yet their shared identity depends on God's continued presence, which means their identity is conditional. If God is with them, they are God's people. But if not, their identity is in question. Moses understands this, and his fear is justified. He recognizes that this is a crucial moment for God's people.

While the golden calf is smoldering, Moses pleads with God to remain with them. He cries, "If your Presence does not go with us, do not send us up from here. How will anyone know that you are pleased with me and with your people unless you go with us? What else will distinguish me and your people from all the other people on the face of the earth?" (Exodus 33:15-16). God responds favorably, and Moses receives detailed instructions. Interestingly, the author frequently describes the Israelites as willing participants in this tabernacle-construction process. Maybe they too realize their identity as God's people is at stake.

The work is complete. They use oil to anoint the table, altars, lampstand, and basin, and consecrate them as holy—for what is merely material is about to host the divine. Imagine the anticipation as Moses confirms the accuracy of their work and declares to all that the tabernacle is ready. "Then the cloud covered the Tent of Meeting, and the glory of the LORD filled the tabernacle" (Exodus 40:34). The Israelites' identity is realized because God's promised presence is with them in this cloud and stays with them during their journeys. "In all the travels of the Israelites, whenever the cloud lifted from above the tabernacle, they would set out; but if the cloud did not lift, they did not set out—until the day it lifted. So the cloud of the LORD was over the tabernacle by day, and fire was in the cloud by night, in the sight of all the Israelites during all their travels" (Exodus 40:36-40).

God dwells with God's people.

Once the tabernacle-carrying Israelites settle in the Promised Land, the transportable host makes way for the temple. This is the permanent place for God's presence among them for a while—until the Babylonians destroy the temple and send the Israelites into exile. Because they are apart from God's presence, their identity is again at risk until the temple is rebuilt years later.

The story line continues, and God's promised presence takes new form. God comes to earth in human flesh: Jesus Christ, baptized by the Spirit, is *Emmanuel*, God dwelling with us. Even when the disciples fear the future without Jesus' presence, the promise continues. How? The Spirit will come upon them. Jesus ensures their identity as God's people because the Spirit "lives with you [plural] and will be in you [plural]. I will not leave you [plural] as orphans" (John 14:17-18). The wind of the Spirit blows at Pentecost and gives birth to Christ's church. God's people are "marked in him with a seal, the promised Holy Spirit, who is a deposit guaranteeing our inheritance [note the plural identity] until the redemption of those who are God's possession" (Ephesians 1:13-14).

Our vital identity is as God's people, Christ's reconciling activity is a vital purpose for relationships, and these relationships are an avenue for the Spirit's powerful transformation. God still dwells among God's people. *Presence* continues to mark our shared identity. Just like Israel, this is our hope.

We are a dwelling place. The "temple of the Holy Spirit" is one of the main New Testament metaphors for the church. It seems today we use the metaphor most commonly to refer to our personal bodies (based loosely on 1 Corinthians 6). This is a powerful way to talk about taking care of our bodies, making responsible moral decisions, or describing the Spirit's transforming work in our individual lives. However, the most frequent use of the metaphor by New Testament authors refers to the community of faith rather than individuals. Just as the temple was God's dwelling place among God's people (2 Chronicles 6:1-2), the church now "hosts" God's presence—with one significant change.

No longer is the focus on a special building; rather, the fellowship of believers is the temple of the Holy Spirit. Paul declares, "In him *you* too are being built together to become a dwelling in which God lives by his Spirit" (Ephesians 2:22). Yes, the *you* in this verse is plural. Paul is describing the community of faith. The church's long and diverse history consistently describes the Spirit's activity in the community. Long ago, Irenaeus, a second-century bishop, writes in *Against Heresies*, "Where the church is, there is also the Spirit of God. And where the Spirit of God is, there is also the church and all grace; for the Spirit is Truth."[7]

A clarification is necessary. I am not saying God is only present in the community. I am saying God's presence is uniquely with *us*. *We* are now the dwelling place for God's presence. We are a temple of the Holy Spirit. Pause for a moment to allow this to enliven your imagination. God is with *us*—*God's people*. Christian communities are never just a supplement for personal faith. The reciprocal community is vital.

The Spirit's presence is our source of power. When the Spirit is at work, the impossible becomes possible. In Ephesians 2, Paul explains the implications of Christ's work on the cross. Clearly, the first-century Christians are trying to wrap their heads around the idea that Christ's resurrection alters the long-standing relationship between Jews and Gentiles. For identity-formed Jews, this must be incredibly disruptive.

Let's also picture the Gentile experience and revisit Ephesians 2. The Gentiles live separated from God's presence by a temple wall that relegates them to the outer court. Their daily lives reinforce the fact that they do not share in the benefits of God's covenant promises. Since Gentiles were unclean according to Jewish law, imagine what it was like for a Gentile to be avoided for fear of contamination. At the time this letter arrives, ethnic tensions are reaching a new level of intensity amid the expanding first-century Roman Empire. For a Gentile identity, tearing down a physical wall is surely more feasible than breaking down these long-standing walls of enmity. How is it possible to thaw this frozen lake? This is the Spirit's work. Paul declares that the inconceivable Jew-Gentile relationship can be reconciled because the two have access to the same Spirit (Ephesians 2:18). This is more than an announcement that things are different. God's presence is with them to actively do more than they can do themselves.

To understand what it's like for a source of power to meet limited humanity, watch superheroes awaken to their identity. In the 2014 television series *The Flash*, the lead character, Barry Allen, or Flash, realizes his extraordinary perception and speed. We watch the *real* become *super*. Viewers are amazed by the unfolding scenes as Barry realizes he can see "evil" in slow motion. When he sees a criminal reaching for a policeman's gun, Barry discovers he is able to move *in a flash* and intervene. He is awakened to a source of power that far exceeds human ability. Power meets his limited humanity.

In a May 7, 2012, article in the *Atlantic* titled, "On the Importance of Having Superheroes," Jen Doll reflects on our cultural fascination with superheroes. Based on the record-breaking success of *The Avengers*, she says, "We want something bigger than us—these are like the steroid fables of our time, the giant, expansive, special-effects-laden lessons through which we can hope to look at humanity and do a little better in human-world." Superhero fascination expresses our longing for superhuman power to help us overcome human limitations in real life. Doll concludes, "The beauty of superheroes is that they're aspirational while at the same time relieving any pressure to actually become a superhero because, well, that's impossible." Christians cannot come to the same conclusion so readily. The Spirit's presence and the inconceivable go hand in hand. Theologian Wolfhart Pannenberg describes the Spirit's power as lifting us out of our limited selves to do what exceeds human ability.[8] For when the Spirit is present, superhuman abilities are possible.

The Spirit's power aligns with God's purposes. A good superhero storyline includes the temptation to use power for good or evil. After all, villains like Batman's Joker and Spider-Man's Green Goblin are evil-choosing superheroes. If the Christian community has access to power through the Spirit, might this lead to arrogance or abuse of power? Yes, it can. Christian history, our history, includes far too many examples of Christians harmfully wielding power. Let us not be naive—this can also be you or me. Many years ago I heard a public figure wisely proclaim that when we point to evil "out there," we should be quick to turn our finger around and point at ourselves first. Christians (you and I) will be tempted to misuse power when we perceive ourselves as in control of the Spirit. If this is the case, power overcoming our limitations is merely an illusion since the source of power will be ourselves. Avoiding this requires vigilant self-examination and accountability. Thankfully, we are not superheroes and do not control the Spirit's power.

The Spirit's presence is the real source of power. Yet this power is never arbitrary or exercised without intention. The Spirit's power has a purpose. Just like you cannot separate me from my actions, so also the Spirit's work aligns with God's purposes. As New Testament scholar David Dockery concludes, Paul understands one of the Spirit's primary purposes as liberation.[9] The Spirit sets us free for the purposes of God. "Now the Lord is the Spirit, and where the Spirit of the Lord is, there is freedom" (2 Corinthians 3:17). We have already examined God's purpose for Christian community. Ultimately, the Spirit will liberate us for God and one another. We will live in a community where our relationships with God and others are fully reconciled. If this is the purpose of the Spirit's presence among us, our church and youth ministry priorities should seek to align with the Spirit's purpose. Relationships within the faith community matter because they are a primary avenue for the Spirit's powerful, liberating activity. We, the church comprised of confessing Christ-followers of all ages, are the temple of the Holy Spirit and are being built into a dwelling place for God. God's presence *with us* in Christ confirms our shared identity, and the Spirit's power is our source for the seemingly impossible call to live as a reconciled people. This is not an abstract idea. The Spirit's movement among us transforms real-life, differing-willed persons.

The church's ongoing transformation proclaims God's redeeming love for all creation. This is the vision of a reciprocal church. We have quite the challenge before us. Theologian Veli-Matti Kärkkäinen captures the importance of this vision and warns, "How well—or poorly— the Christian church is

> **Relationships within the faith community matter because they are a primary avenue for the Spirit's powerful, liberating activity.**

able to fulfill this basic task determines to a large extent how relevant the church is going to be for the third millennium."[10] It is time to talk about the values and practices that will keep us on this path. How do we live into the Spirit's liberating activity and become a community where faith flourishes into adulthood?

PART 2

VALUES AND PRACTICES FOR FLOURISHING COMMUNITIES

6

TETHERBALL AND FLOODLIGHTS

VALUING MEMORY

T'S HOMECOMING DAY. Clusters of people line all sides of the quad, a beautiful field and central gathering point on campus. As I make my way through the crowds, I watch similar scenes echo across the wide age span, from recent graduates to alumni celebrating their golden reunion. It goes something like this. "Remember when we accidentally set fire to the trash can at 2 a.m.?" "Remember when we stayed up all night to study for that philosophy exam, and the next morning discovered we showed up a day early?" "Remember when our friend fell off the cliff and spent weeks in the ICU?" "Remember when we protested outside the president's office, and he just opened the window and sent us back to class?" "Remember when you made that buzzer-beater basket during the championship game?" As old friends get reacquainted, the awkwardness quickly slips away beneath shared memories. Similarly, youth groups thrive on stories. "Remember when Greg backed the van into the wall?" "Remember when Genevieve left her passport on the plane?" "Remember when we played capture the flag in the snow?" Stories build a common memory.

Facebook knows the power of memory. This omniscient platform provides pictures from years ago and kindly invites us to share the memory in our virtual community. I have a good friend who takes pleasure in posting and reposting a picture of us from high school. Yes, it is the one when I mistimed my smile. Each time she posts it, I laugh and experience a flood of "remember when" moments. Our lives take form around stories. Stories (for both good and ill) tell us who we are and where we come from. Shared memories tell us we belong. In a similar way, faith forms around shared stories. When stories from the Bible intersect with our present lives, we become part of Christianity's "remember when" story. We belong. When memory becomes important to a community, it becomes a reciprocal church. But what kind of memory? Understanding our memory begins by defining God's memory.

> **When stories from the Bible intersect with our present lives, we become part of Christianity's "remember when" story.**

GOD'S MEMORY

All-knowing memory. Remembering intersects with a description of God as *omniscient*, which means "all-knowing." God's omniscience includes complete knowledge of the past, present, and future. Unlike any counterpart in creation, God knows all even before it comes to be and long after it passes away. All is simultaneously present to God. God's memory in this sense is a totality. This conception of God is a hope we cling to. When the future is uncertain or unstable, we take comfort in the fact that God is all-knowing. I sometimes grimace when Christians use cliché phrases like "God is still seated on the throne" or "It will all work out in the end." Yet even if overused or needing nuance, we cling to these expressions because they speak to our deepest hope. God is greater than we are and is redeeming all things through Christ Jesus. God's memory extends before, within, and beyond the moment, and this provokes our trust and hope.

Responsive memory. Yet God as all-knowing is not a complete characterization of the Christian God. Omniscience emphasizes God as *distinct* from creation, but this attribute alone does not describe God's relationship *with* creation. Theologian Stanley Grenz reminds us that even at the height of theologians articulating God as omniscient, omnipotent, and omnipresent, the early Christian churches also continued to worship God as responsive and compassionate.[1] They were expressing their experiences with God and the witness of God's people throughout the biblical stories. In the Old Testament, when authors refer to God "remembering," this generally involves far more than things coming to mind, because God is all-knowing. Repeatedly, remembering for the biblical authors entails God taking action or responding favorably. Because God remembers the covenant with Noah, signified by the rainbow (Genesis 9:15), God's future protection is trustworthy. When God remembers the promise made to the Hebrews, God frees them from enslavement in Egypt (Exodus 2:24). Rachel (Genesis 30:22) and Hannah (1 Samuel 1:19) each conceive after God remembers they are barren. As God remembers errant Samson, he gains victory over the Philistines (Judges 16:28). These stories tell us how responsiveness is part of God's memory.

While God's omniscience exceeds the limits of time and space, God's memory acts within human history. These two seemingly contradictory conceptions of God actually live in dynamic tension. Isolating God's eternality ignores God's compassion and responsiveness. Conversely, isolating God's present action among us minimizes God's eternality and sovereignty. Listen to how these attributes come together when the psalmist declares that God "remembers his covenant forever" (Psalms 105:8). *Forever* is God's omniscience and *covenant* marks God's faithful response to us.

Memory is for relationship. Descriptions of God's memory are often tied to the covenants.[2] In Old Testament theology, covenants establish the relationship between God and God's people. When the biblical authors describe God remembering a covenant, it is generally because God's people have forgotten to keep up their end of the deal. When God "remembers," this frequently includes *extending mercy* to them because God seeks to maintain this relationship. For example, Isaiah declares to wayward Israel, God "remembers your sins no more" (Isaiah 43:18-19, 25), and the prophet Jeremiah compares God's remembering to a parent's deep love:

> Is not Ephraim my dear son,
>   the child in whom I delight?
> Though I often speak against him,
>   I still remember him.
> Therefore my heart yearns for him;
>   I have great compassion for him. (Jeremiah 31:20)

Because relationship is essential to God, God's all-knowing memory of the covenant alone is insufficient. While God's omniscience includes all that is or will be, God's memory is simultaneously responsive and relationally committed—to us.

Memory is trustworthy: God is faithful. It is clear that God's "remember when" moments do not always paint a pretty picture of Israel. In fact, when Israel is the subject of remembering, they usually fall short.[3] "You [Israel] have not remembered the Rock" (Isaiah 17:10). This does not surprise us because, like Israel, we too tend to forget. God remembers their "wickedness" because "they greatly love to wander; / they do not restrain their feet" (Jeremiah 14:10). This indictment points back to God's relational memory because the Israelites are guilty of wandering away from the covenant. Surely Israel's forgetfulness is not overlooked. God will remember their sins (Hosea 9:9), and judgment awaits Babylon because "God remembered her crimes" (Revelation 18:5).[4]

Yet, when God remembers Israel's inability to remain faithful, a responsive and relationship-preserving act is not far behind. God is the one who remains faithful. Old Testament scholar Ronald Hendel says memory in the Bible is "the account of the actions of God on behalf of the people."[5] Memory is faithfulness. Hear the psalmist reflect on God's memory alongside an honest recognition of human frailty: "[God] remembered that they were but flesh, / a passing breeze that does not return" (Psalm 78:39). God remembers in our "low estate" (Psalm 136:23). Memory of our unfaithfulness elicits God's faithfulness as Paul affirms that while we were stuck in our sin, "Christ died for the ungodly" (Romans 5:6). The psalmists repeatedly give praise and thanks for God's trustworthy memory:

> Sing to the LORD a new song,
>> for he has done marvelous things;
> his right hand and his holy arm
>> have worked salvation for him.
> The LORD has made his salvation known
>> and revealed his righteousness to the nations.
> He has *remembered* his love
>> and his faithfulness to Israel;
> all the ends of the earth have seen
>> the salvation of our God. (Psalm 98:1-3; italics added)

Even in grief-filled cries for help, the hope that God will remember and be faithful persists:

> O God, why have you rejected us forever?
>> Why does your anger smolder against the sheep of your
>>> pasture?
> *Remember* the nation you purchased long ago,
>> the people of your inheritance, whom you redeemed—
> Mount Zion, where you dwelt.
>> (Psalm 74:1-2; italics added)

Memory is our hope. God's all-knowing memory is a totality, and all is simultaneously present to God. Maintainer of our covenant relationship, God's memory includes responsive acts in human history that preserve our relationship with God. We too have such stories. God is faithful because God remembers. God's memory is essential for redemption. It is a mark of God's faithfulness—and is therefore trustworthy.

Our memory: A people belonging to God. We are one of *those* groups. Standing in the airport hallway blocking people as they rush to make their flights. We are wearing the same T-shirt (a.k.a. self-imposed humiliation) and counting off from 1 to 50. Do you recognize the scene? Leaving a kid behind is a nightmare I fear while awake. I have no trouble imagining the sick feeling that accompanies the realization that someone in my care is missing. In college, we leave a young woman behind after touring the Aztec ruins near Mexico City. It takes six long, anxious hours to locate her. On one of our infamous ski trips (and before cell phones), two kids think it would be fun to see if we noticed their absence and hide in a store while the bus pulls onto the highway. An hour later, the bus driver makes a frantic U-turn (or is that me who is frantic?). Such experiences explain why we are standing in everyone's way in the airport using the annoying, yet dependable, counting system. Our memories are weak. We forget.

I am always on the lookout for the latest reminder app. Surely someone will create an app that will be able to *remember* when I *forget* to input an appointment. We forget to pay bills and send birthday wishes to people we deeply love. We are a forgetful people. Here is the good news: Christianity depends on God's memory. God does not forget. Amid our inability to remember, God remains faithful. We find hope in the inextricable connection between God's memory and

Here is the good news: Christianity depends on God's memory. God does not forget.

faithfulness. Yet this does not rid us of responsibility. When we remember, we too will be faithful. But when we forget, we are prone to wander.

In Deuteronomy we read many commands to remember as well as warnings not to forget. The Israelites receive a timely instruction when they are about to enter the land of Canaan. They know there is danger ahead of them because they are about to face their enemies. However, there is a greater danger. "Be careful that you do not *forget* the LORD your God, failing to observe his commands, his laws and his decrees that I am giving you this day" (Deuteronomy 8:11; italics added). If the Israelites forget, this will result in being unfaithful to their covenant with God. There is good news though. God provides a remembering plan. "Remember that you were slaves in Egypt and that the LORD your God brought you out of there with a mighty hand and an outstretched arm. Therefore the LORD your God has commanded you to observe the Sabbath day" (Deuteronomy 5:15). There are two steps to this remembering plan: (1) fill your memories with stories of God's faithfulness, such as God freeing the Hebrews from slavery, and (2) practice remembering by keeping the Sabbath. Proclaiming God's faithfulness and the Sabbath join because we need to practice remembering. *A reciprocal church values memory by retelling our family story as God's people and makes remembering a central practice in its community's life.*

MEMORY: A TETHER IN THE PRESENT

Prone to ignore the past. Valuing memory is easier said than done. Not only are we forgetful, but we also find that resisting the past may be more appealing. I say this for two reasons. First, we live in a rapidly changing world due, in part, to the technological advances all around us. The quality of our lives has certainly improved due to these developments. Surgeons use robotic arms to carry out less invasive and more intricate surgeries. Engineers build alternative energy sources that can reduce our environmental footprint. The developing world benefits from advanced communication networks. The list of benefits goes on and on.

In addition to these significant advantages, we also face unintended consequences. Technological advances can increase and intensify the pace of change in our daily lives. We turn our attention to what it enables now. For example, our smartphones always need updating. In order to use new apps and games or connect to our banks, we have to keep up with the latest operating system. In many ways, we are locked into structures that require us to "need" the latest model since what is new quickly becomes obsolete. Social media has forever changed the way we relate to one another. Whether your social media platform is Twitter, LinkedIn, Facebook, or Instagram (and others created since the publication of this book), being active in these platforms demands our attention and becomes a priority. Young people feel this acutely, for if they are not "seen" in the digital space they may be forgotten. "Who I am" feels like it is constantly negotiated in fleeting digital appearances rather than through long-standing relationships. From the latest gaming systems to shopping online to methods of payment, the regular drumbeat of our lives includes keeping up with our changing world. This requires us to orient our time, priorities, money, and interests toward the future for fear of being left behind. We can easily turn our backs on the past and forget the histories and heritages that inform our identities.

Second, it is also easier to resist the past because our relationship with history feels cloudy right now. We are working hard to incorporate more perspectives into our historical narratives. For example, *Christianity Today* ran a moving article in 2017 titled "Facing Our Legacy of Lynching." D. L. Mayfield powerfully explains the ongoing efforts to uncover this part of America's tragic history: "More than 4,000 African Americans were lynched between 1877 and the rise of the civil rights movement in the early 1950s."[6] Yet these individual stories are largely unknown. Advocacy groups such as the Equal Justice Initiative (EJI) work to help us remember these stories, for, as Mayfield rightly declares, "Buried sins cannot be repented of." In 2018 a memorial will be built in downtown Montgomery, Alabama, inscribed with the names of four thousand men, women, and children who were killed along with the eight hundred different counties in the United States where lynchings took place. When we do not remember, we forget.

We are increasingly aware of the need to examine and enlarge our history, which is why our relationship with history feels cloudy right now. This is as true for the way we tell the history of the United States as it is for our recounting of Christianity's story. Refining our history is hard work requiring confession, forgiveness, sharing power, and reconciliation. We are still negotiating how to do this without also further dividing our already polarized country and churches.[7] If we are honest, it is much easier to resist the past, fortify our memory as it is—or just forget. It is tempting to allow technology's alluring rapid pace of change to turn us toward the future and ignore the past. We could all just decide to live in Snapchat where our history expires after twenty-four hours.

But don't forget, we serve a God whose memory is essential for redemption and calls us to remember.

Untethered. In 1998, psychologist David Elkind was already telling us that young people were facing increased stress. He defines stress as "our response to an *extraordinary* demand for adaptation."[8] Add the distinct features of the twenty-first century such as technology's acceleration

> **It is tempting to allow technology's alluring rapid pace of change to turn us toward the future and ignore the past.**

of change, examination of our history, and living in a pluralistic culture, and the pressure for young people to adapt to change only increases. The American Academy of Pediatrics published the results of a study on adolescent depression in 2016.[9] Over a twelve-month period, young people who report experiencing one depression episode was up 37 percent. Researchers conclude, "Major depression is one of the deadliest diseases among adolescents and is associated with the rise in self-injury among teenagers." Their findings also reveal that girls are particularly vulnerable. Developmental researcher Belle Liang confirms that even affluent adolescent girls who we have thought were low risk are exhibiting increased psychological stress.[10] *Time* magazine's 2016 cover page captures the recent flood of research with a lead article titled "Teen Depression and Anxiety: Why the Kids Are Not Alright."[11] Although we await research confirming exact causes, psychologist Jean Twenge studies trends in standard surveys. She alerts us to the convincing correlation between increased screen use and stress among emerging generations.[12] In a recent article in the *Atlantic* she says, "The more time teens spend looking at screens, the more likely they are to report symptoms of depression."[13]

Social media newsfeeds expose young people to a drumbeat of future global threats. Last week I overheard a middle school girl expressing her fears to an adult. What does she fear most? The United States being bombed. Screens open wide doors to a world of unfiltered information with a new category called "fake news." More information exasperates fears (whether real or not) and expands our options and choices. From our coffees to schools to fast-food chains to churches, our daily lives require endless decision making. In a 2006 *Harvard Business Review* article, Barry Schwartz examines the impact of increased choices on personal satisfaction in fields from psychology to business. Too many choices can result in "choice paralysis." He warns that having more to choose from "requires increased time and effort and can lead to anxiety, regret, excessively high expectations, and self-blame if the choices don't work out."[14] Growing up today is uniquely stressful.

There is a disturbing scene at the beginning of the 2013 movie *Gravity*. Dr. Ryan Stone, played by Sandra Bullock, is on her first shuttle mission. We watch her confidently carry out a routine spacewalk while repairing the Hubble Space Telescope. The peaceful experience does not last as a debris field strikes the shuttle. For one minute and fifteen seconds, we experience her utter terror of being untethered from the spacecraft, swirling in space. Desperately trying to locate her, Mission Control calls out, "Give me a visual. Do you have a visual of

Explorer? Do you have a visual of ISS? You need a focus! Anything—the sun or the earth. Give me coordinates! Give me coordinates!" No orientation. No tether. Detached and swirling in space.

I wonder if this is what it feels like to be a young person today. Might the increased demand for adaptation, constant phone notifications, and limitless choices coupled with our tendency to resist the past leave young people untethered and swirling in space?

Tetherballs. I remember growing up in the desert sands of El Paso, Texas. The elementary school playground includes the typical equipment plus some "perks." We are experts at going down the slides without our legs or hands touching the burning hot metal. The baseball backstop is a perfect location for catching scorpions, and the deep desert sand cushions our landing as we launch off the swings. A fourth-grade favorite is the tetherball. A long line forms at recess as we each try to unseat the week's champion. Tetherball is the perfect elementary school game because it has a built-in safeguard for the uncoordinated among us (or is that all of us?). Unlike volleyball or basketball, there are no missed balls to chase, which would slow down the pace of the game. The tethered ball means tons of uninterrupted action even if there is an occasional bloody nose.

The most common definition of *tether* has a negative connotation—"to restrain." We tether animals to restrict movement or to rein them in. Yet it also means "to secure," which implies the need to stabilize, ground, or safeguard. Because the ball is tethered to the pole, we have freedom to actually play the game. To be a Christian is to be tethered to our shared identity as God's people. We are able to trust in God's memory because God always remembers and is faithful. Memory is a tether for young people. It secures them (and us) and provides a point of orientation in a changing world.

Remembering is to belong. Valuing memory is evident in Nehemiah. Ezra and Nehemiah are historical books that take place after

Babylon conquers the southern kingdom of Israel—Judah. As a result, large numbers of Jerusalem's citizens are sent into exile in Babylon, and destruction falls on the city and the temple. The Israelites live as refugees for sixty to seventy years. This means an entire generation is living in captivity. Imagine the memory implications: no access to the temple, no participation in annual feasts, no making sacrifices, and no reading of the Law of Moses (likely a portion of the Torah). These people are untethered from their story and they forget.

But God remembers. The Persians conquer the Babylonians. Cyrus, a Persian King, declares it is time for the refugees among them to return to Jerusalem. In the book of Ezra we read about the first wave of those who return. The people successfully rebuild the temple, and Ezra, a priest and scribe, leads a spiritual renewal, calling people to spiritual, social, and political repentance. Another wave of people return to Jerusalem under Nehemiah's leadership and rebuild the city wall. When Nehemiah 8 opens, the wall is complete, and people are resettling in the city. Now it is time to reinstitute the practice of Torah reading.

It is the seventh day (when the civil year begins), and all are gathered in the square. Women and children are not typically invited. But on special occasions like this one, everyone is present. Palpable excitement fills the air as even the squirmiest kid among them stands still in anticipation of this moment. Ezra stands high on a purposefully designed platform with Nehemiah and the Levites (instructors of the Law). Before the expectant crowd, Ezra declares his praise to "the great God." A thunderous roar follows from the crowd, "Amen! Amen!" They bow down and press their faces to the ground in worship of God. The leaders read from the lost Torah as the Levites move intentionally through the crowd "making it clear and giving the meaning so that the people could understand what was being read" (Nehemiah 8:8).

As the people rediscover their history, sounds of weeping and mourning echo through the assembly. Why? They realize they are untethered. They have forgotten *who they are* and *where they come from*. Maybe shame or guilt evokes this dramatic response. Without access to these readings, their memory has faded. Maybe this is when they are first aware that they are not fulfilling the Law's requirements. Forgetting leads to unfaithfulness. I also wonder if this is an expression of grief. Not only do they discover the Law, but they also discover who they are and the story they belong to. Might they also be overwhelmed by the lost time and missed family connections? Ezra, Nehemiah, and the Levites quickly intervene and declare a celebration. What matters today is that they now know who they are and where they come from. Making sure that this time no one is left out of the story, Nehemiah says, "Go and enjoy choice food and sweet drinks, and send some to those who have nothing prepared. This day is holy to our Lord" (Nehemiah 8:10). Why should they celebrate? Because God's memory is faithful—God remembers. When these people remember, their identities retether to this story. Once again, they belong.

My dad's side of the family, the Galgays, takes our lineage rather seriously. Both of my grandparents are of Irish immigrant heritage and, like many others, faced significant obstacles. Grandpa became a federal judge, and Grandma graduated from a prestigious college long before this is commonplace for women. Galgays stand on the shoulders of an inspiring patriarch and matriarch who model life lived well: work hard and love hard. Even today, these stories tether my identity, reminding me *who I am and where I come from*.

We discover a problem. My generation of Galgays notice that our kids are unfamiliar with the family stories and fear these stories will die with us. Faithful to our Irish roots, we gather for a weekend of storytelling (a.k.a. we practice remembering). There are endless "remember when" tales, and we revel as the accumulated memories, which are surely mixed with exaggerated folklore, come to life.

Weeks later, my daughter comes home from school with a drawing curiously signed, "Annie Galgay." Galgay is not her last name. For the next two months, every math page, vocabulary test, trombone practice sheet, and piece of artwork proudly displays the Galgay signature. Learning the family stories tethers—secures rather than restricts—Annie's identity. She is a Galgay. Like the Israelites, she discovers who she is and where she comes from. She belongs to a story larger than herself.

Shared identity and adolescent development. Identity formation is central to human development. In the 2006 edition of the *Handbook of Child Psychology*, W. Andres Collins and Laurence Steinberg describe a significant change in the approach to studying adolescent identity development among contemporary researchers.[15] Historically, research focused on the individual person's identity formation and measured development through categories such as personal achievement, competence, and self-esteem. These researchers did not ignore a young person's surrounding environment (family, school, peers, etc.), but the focus remained only on the *changing person* rather than the person's *changing relationships* with others.

Western conceptions of maturity reinforce this framework. Generally, maturity encompasses a person's ability to individuate or define self through separation. This is distinct from a typical (yet not exclusive) Eastern emphasis on "interpersonal competence and social interconnection."[16] Imagine the implications. A Western teenager's main developmental task is to figure out who they are and stand on their own two feet: independent and separate.

Collins and Steinberg describe more recent research trajectories that are expanding these earlier conceptions. Identity forms as young people separate themselves from others *and* as they simultaneously form connections with others. The two cannot be separated. They write, "The development of autonomy almost always implies independence *from or in relation to* some person (e.g., a parent), group, or institution."[17] Consequently, both independence (who I am) and interdependence (who I am with others) are adolescent developmental tasks. Relationships with others are a crucial aspect of development.

Faith and belonging. To be a Christian is to join with others. We are a people belonging to God. We frequently say we want kids to "take faith on as their own." But doesn't a maturing faith include more than separation? Since Christians have a shared identity, maturing faith must also include an evolving relationship with the community. This emphasis supports healthy adolescent development by affording them the opportunity to negotiate self with others. Particularly today, young people need a community's memory to tether them in a changing world. I am not saying that our inherited stories are always a gift. Those returning from exile in Nehemiah found a history wrought with unfaithfulness. Our family histories and church traditions are no different. I am saying that we need to heed the remembering plan suggested in Deuteronomy 5:15. First, fill your memories with stories of God's faithfulness, and second, practice remembering. These experiences will act as a securing tether and hopefully reduce the stress young people are experiencing in our rapidly changing world. And more, the Christian story in all its messy forgetfulness finds hope not in our own memory but in God's memory. God remembers and is faithful. Helping young people develop a connection with the community should be a top priority in churches.

MEMORY: A FLOODLIGHT FOR THE FUTURE

Securing teenagers is not the ultimate end. In fact, when we focus on securing their faith, our motivations can quickly dissolve into fears that their faith won't stick. We provide a tether so that young people are *free* to become actors in the Christian story. Let's turn back to Nehemiah.

The Israelites gather for another day and discover an important "remember when" story. On that day, "they found written in the Law, which the LORD had commanded through Moses, that the Israelites were to live in temporary shelters during the festival of the seventh month" (Nehemiah 8:14). It is time for the Feast of Tabernacles or Succoth, a seven-day festival in which the Israelites live in temporary shelters to commemorate God's bringing them out of Egypt. They scatter in search of needed materials and shelters called booths or tents. They lay branches across the top and create small openings, which expose the sky. Sleeping here and gazing up at the stars will remind them of God's faithfulness in the wilderness. These people are literally acting out their forgotten story.

It is easy to see how the past is shaping their identity. This is a hands-on learning experience. Participating in the past tethers their present; they experience belonging while they practice remembering. Yet this account is more than duplication. Something unique just happened. The detailed descriptions in this remembering event in Nehemiah 8 are not in the Leviticus account (Leviticus 23:40-43). You see, as they remember their story, they also become actors in it. They discover who they are and where they come from, and this inaugurates their future as they build memories together by making tents with holes in the roofs. "The whole company that had returned from exile built temporary shelters and lived in them. From the days of Joshua son of Nun until that day, the Israelites had not celebrated it like this. And their joy was very great" (Nehemiah 8:17).

Young people as innovators. New Testament scholar N. T. Wright's analogy of a "fifth act play" best captures the connection between our memories and the future. Wright proposes a scenario where the fifth act of a Shakespearian play is lost, and a group of actors are asked to "work out the fifth act for themselves."[18] He presses us to understand two requirements for this task: consistency and innovation. First, the actors need to learn the first four acts. If they don't solidify their understanding of what has already occurred, the fifth act will make no sense and may even begin a new play. The actors must discover threads within the first four acts to carry throughout the play so the fifth act is *consistent* with the preceding acts. And yet, if they arrive on stage and only perform what already happened—overly concerned with consistency—there will be no fifth act. The actors must now innovate. Tethered by acts 1-4, they are now free to perform the fifth act. Wright describes the church to be like the fifth-act performers. And we know young people are certainly able actors.

Our memory is identity shaping, tethering us to God's people and, in turn, enabling us to be actors in God's unfolding drama. A floodlight along a dark road helps a person see what is ahead. It does not erase the surrounding darkness or shadows but provides enough light to discern a way forward. Christians do not create *ex nihilo*. We innovate in a manner consistent with the Christian story. It takes a lot of remembering practice to know the story we join. The Bible is not a handbook that provides specific answers to every tension found when faith and life conflict. Like

> **A church's memory acts as a floodlight for young people to become actors in God's redemptive history as it unfolds.**

the Israelites' innovative tent constructions, a church's memory also acts as a floodlight for young people to become actors in God's redemptive history as it unfolds.

PRACTICE REMEMBERING

Pay attention to the church year. Calendars structure and organize. Every week my husband and I look carefully at each day to make sure we coordinate our busy lives. Between two jobs and two active kids, the calendar keeps us sane (and reminds us to pick up the kids). Calendars create structure. They begin and end and have a known cycle in between. The school calendar begins at the end of summer, breaks into two or three semesters, holds regular breaks, and then ends. We pay attention to the IRS's calendar when we scramble to pull together needed documents before taxes are due. I know a church that calendars everything in consultation with the University of Tennessee football schedule (Go Vols). Calendars establish a rhythm in our lives and help us remember when we forget.

I am in a class of upperclassmen examining a simple calendar representing the church year. These students come from a wide range of traditions: Pentecostals, Roman Catholics, Baptists, Presbyterians, and the span of nondenominationals. My lecture takes an unexpected turn. Over and over, their expressions of dismay fill the room. "I didn't know what Lent was until I came to college." "When I was a freshman, I thought Black Friday was the same as Good Friday." "The Ascension was news to me." And these are only the events surrounding Easter. A Roman Catholic student has a different response. "In my parish, we rely on the church calendar. This is how I understand myself as a Christian." That's it. Calendars organize and provide a structure for our story. Search for resources to help your church practice remembering such as the seasonal focused books in the *Let Us Keep the Feast* series.[19]

Here is another idea: download an app for the church year. Pick two moments from across the church year that your church typically does not recognize. Look for natural connections to what you are already doing rather than adding in an obscure day. How will you practice remembering? Ask the pastor to talk about these in the sermon. Note the representative colors and find a way to add them to the decor. Do your research and reenact the event as a whole church or in community groups. Be creative as you strive for both consistency *and* innovation.

Change the lyrics. You knew this was coming, didn't you? My husband is a gifted worship leader. He takes great care choosing music to help design our worship gatherings. He wants his efforts to facilitate a community's common voice. Sometimes we express praise or thanksgiving and at other times confession or lament. Rummaging through contemporary worship music dominated by words like *I, me,* and *my* makes this a rather difficult task. How might our worship gatherings change, in message and experience, if lyrics shifted into the plural? After all, *we* are singing these words when we gather.

We are at a beautiful retreat center on the Maine shoreline. Fifty women are graciously listening to me and grappling with our shared identity. Four talented women lead singing before each session. I know the damage I can cause by mentioning my frustration with the individual-centered lyrics, so I do not use this example with the group. At dinner on Saturday night, one of the worship leaders whispers that she has a surprise for me. She tells me that as they practiced their song set, something seemed off. They wonder, "How can we be singing about *me* while embracing our shared identity?" They start altering lyrics, and the result blows me away. Here is an excerpt from the song "I Need You." The song is written as a personal confession saying, "Lord, I need you." Imagine singing this as God's people and confessing *our* need for God.

> Without You *we* fall apart
> You're the One that guides *our* hearts
> Lord, *we* need You.[20]

"Without you we fall apart." Christian communities need to sing this prayer together. God is forming a people, a body, a temple—a sign pointing to what one day we will be in the ultimate community. Plural lyrics help us remember what we easily forget. They help us resist our habit of consuming God and one another. We underestimate the forming power of the words we sing. John Wesley once said that lyrics are the greatest theological education people receive in the church. This is not a call to go back to hymns or to denigrate contemporary worship songs. In fact, there are many talented musicians writing songs that enable us to practice remembering who *we* are as we sing. Healthy adolescent development includes a changing relationship with others. Singing words that emphasize our shared identity will become real time memories of being God's people.

Connect the dots. When I pick up a book I have read in search of a salient quote or poignant dialogue, I can approximate where to find it. Books have visual beginnings, middles, and endings. What happens when your entire life is spent reading the Bible on a smartphone, tablet, or computer screen? Searching and sorting on our devices is surely advantageous. But how would you know where to find the middle of the story? Memory of a story requires knowing the flow of events along the way. There is plenty of compelling research crossing our Twitter feeds to remind us of an epidemic. Biblical illiteracy is pervasive. Confusion about Peter's role in the story versus Moses is only clarified when we connect the dots into the broader story line.

Commit to *never* (that is a strong word) teaching a section of Scripture without connecting it to the larger narrative of Scripture. The following is an example of how to do this from the Nehemiah we have already looked at.

In the Jewish tradition the books Ezra and Nehemiah are one book intended to be read together. These books tell of a crucial moment in God's covenant relationship with Israel. This is the covenant initiated by God with Abraham where God promises to "make [him] into a great nation" through which "all the peoples on earth will be blessed" (Genesis 12:2-3). The great nation is Israel, and their long history is marked by unfaithfulness, but is followed by God calling wayward Israel back into this covenant relationship through (or in spite of) different priests, kings, and especially the prophets. This covenantal relationship anticipates redemption through Jesus Christ's life, death, and resurrection, the birth of the Christian church at Pentecost, and ultimately the restoration of all creation.

God's memory and ours. Memory is powerful. Young people who are maturing in faith do not only take faith on "as their own" as if maturing in faith only means separation. They also need a story to wrap their identities around in our rapidly changing world. When a community values memory, young people know who they are and where they come from because they belong to God's story. The first question and answer of the Heidelberg Catechism makes this clear: "What is [our] only comfort in life and in death? That [we are] not [our] own but belong, body and soul, both in life and in death, unto [our] faithful Saviour Jesus Christ."[21]

This is our hope for one reason: God remembers. God's memory makes way for redemption. We forget, but God's memory is faithful. Let's practice remembering and unveil this identity-shaping, tethering memory for young people because they too are actors in this story. Memory will then act as a floodlight opening up a pathway for the future.

THE OXPECKER'S GIFT

VALUING MUTUALITY

B IOLOGISTS USE THE TERM *mutualism* to describe the relationship between different species living in the same environment. Over time, they learn how to live together, so each benefits from the other, which often ensures their survival. For example, in Africa you will see the yellow or red-billed oxpecker birds riding atop a rhino's back and using their long, thin beaks to feast on ticks and small insects. The rhino supplies needed food for the oxpecker and in return receives a bath. If a rhino has a wound, the oxpeckers will peck it clean by eating parasites that are harmful to the rhino yet nourishing to the birds. What endangers one gives life to the other. You might also see an oxpecker suddenly shoot up in the air screeching loudly to alert the rhino of impending danger. These two creatures demonstrate *mutualism*. They have an interdependent relationship, and both benefit from having the other around.

Like the oxpecker and rhino, we too should benefit from being together. Mutuality emerges as a vital value for Christian communities based on our identity and purpose. As we already explored, knowing our shared identity will help us recapture the meaning of two common words we use to describe Christian community: *fellowship* and *body*. We are *held* in fellowship by Christ. We might be prone to use personal satisfaction as a measuring stick for Christian fellowship. But feeling good about each other and having things in common will come and go. Once we confess this tendency, we are then free to recognize Christ—and only Christ—as the center and source of our fellowship. Christ through the Spirit's power generates and maintains our interdependence. In addition, understanding the body metaphor, especially in the Pauline Epistles, explains *who we are* as a people and not *what we have* like a possession. Paul says, "Now you are the body of Christ, and each one of you is a part of it" (1 Corinthians 12:27). Our shared identity as Christ's body establishes our interdependence but does not magically make this our experience with each other. By implication, our common identity awaits actualization.

If God's ultimate purposes include each of us enjoying right relationships with God and others, then living into our interdependence should be prioritized. Relationships are a primary avenue for transformation and where the Spirit's power does the unimaginable. Like the oxpecker and rhino, we should benefit from having the other around. New Testament scholar James Howard calls this the "solidarity of the redeemed community." Solidarity "refers to the catalytic effect of Christians working together and causing growth to maturity in each other."[1] Solidarity is our interdependence in action. We—you, me, and us—mature from being with one another. As Paul writes, "From him the whole body, joined and held together by every supporting ligament, grows and builds itself up in love, as each part does its work" (Ephesians 4:16). The reciprocal church values mutuality by prizing our *interdependence* because *we are in this together*.

The Way is a 2010 drama written by Emilio Estevez and starring his father, Martin Sheen, who plays the main character, Thomas Avery. The movie opens with Thomas receiving the terrible news that his adult son died during a storm while walking the Camino de Santiago. The Camino, which means "the way," is a well-known spiritual pilgrimage route beginning in France and ending at a cathedral in Spain. Thomas flies to France to gather his son's belongings and ashes. Overcome with grief, he impulsively decides to walk the trail to honor his son. His demeanor makes it clear to all that he is making this journey alone. He resists offers of advice, food, and company. His physical and emotional isolation underscore his pilgrimage. When someone steals his backpack—home to his son's ashes—he frantically chases the person and finds the contents of his backpack strewn across a riverbank. Exhausted and overcome by grief, his body gives way to uncontrollable tears. We experience his sorrow compounded by profound loneliness. As I take in this scene, I am sure he can go no farther.

Enter three persistent fellow pilgrims. For the remainder of the movie, they literally will not leave Thomas alone even as he tries to get rid of them. Each is walking the pilgrimage to work through different life struggles. They discover they need each other. Or maybe Thomas discovers he needs them. The companionship of strangers becomes each person's avenue for healing. Once again someone steals Thomas's backpack. This time three fellow pilgrims join his desperate pursuit not only to reclaim his son's ashes and belongings, but also because they understand Thomas's pain and how the bag binds him to his son. Thomas needs other pilgrims to walk this path of grief with him, and they each need Thomas to walk with them. Our individualistic social world produces people who imagine it is more valiant to figure out life alone; they consider needing help to be a weakness. God's intent for Christian community is a stark contrast. We share an identity and purpose. We need each other—adults and young people alike. Valuing mutuality challenges us to actualize our interdependence.

DIFFERENCE IS OPPORTUNITY

I have spent the majority of this book emphasizing our shared identity and common life in Christ. By God's initiative, we are a people belonging to God and existing for God's purposes. However, interdependence highlights our differences as much as what we have in common. Picture Pixar's *Nemo*. The clownfish and sea anemone's mutualistic relationship depend on something inherent in each creature. The sea anemone's long, poisonous tentacles can conceal the vibrant orange-and-white-striped clownfish from predators. While hiding away, the clownfish consumes unwanted parasites and says thanks for the snack by leaving nutrient-rich excrement for the anemone. Other fish cannot benefit from the tentacles, because they would be stung, but a layer of mucus covers the clownfish and provides needed protection. Similarly, other coral in the ocean do not cover the clownfish like the long, flowing sea anemone's tentacles. It appears each creature is uniquely created to benefit the other. There is something integral to a clownfish and something different that is integral to a sea anemone so their differences become the avenue for their interdependence.

In her 2004 book *Practicing Passion*, Kenda Creasy Dean describes how young people and struggling churches need each other. Without using the word *mutualism*, she describes exactly this.[2] What do churches lack? Passion. What do youth have in abundance? Passion. What do young people lack? Wisdom and experience. What rich resources do churches have? Wisdom and experience. It is as if each is uniquely made to benefit the other. Being young and full of ideals is exactly what churches, often filled with tired or even cynical adults, need to thrive and vice versa. Most disruptions in the church stem from our differences, whether these are preferences, ideas, or experiences. We often gravitate toward what we have in common and avoid leaning into difference. When a community values mutuality, differences can become opportunities. Paul's detailed description of the relationship among the body parts says it clearly.

> The eye cannot say to the hand, "I don't need you!" And the head cannot say to the feet, "I don't need you!" On the contrary, those parts of the body that seem to be weaker are indispensable,

and the parts that we think are less honorable we treat with special honor. And the parts that are unpresentable are treated with special modesty, while our presentable parts need no special treatment. But God has put the body together, giving greater honor to the parts that lacked it, so that there should be no division in the body, but that its parts should have equal concern for each other. If one part suffers, every part suffers with it; if one part is honored, every part rejoices with it. (1 Corinthians 12:21-26)

The passage also outlines how we live together with our differences. We act in ways that ensure all the parts are honored, cared for, and valued. In what ways do we treat young people as indispensable to our churches? If we are in this together, how might we value young people as they are and not just focus on what we want for them?

When a community values mutuality, differences can become opportunities.

MUTUALITY NOT SYMBIOSIS

I am using mutuality to stress interdependence rather than symbiosis. A symbiotic relationship involves one species acting as a host to another. Sometimes these are mutualistic, where both benefit, and at other times the relationship is positive for only one, like a parasite living off its host. Many symbiotic relationships in nature involve one organism physically containing the other, and the two may even become a new organism. Without careful observation, the new organism can eclipse the distinctiveness of each.

A colleague recently sent me an article from a Christian magazine in which a scientist explores what we can learn about Christian community from nature. The author moves beyond more common examples where survival of the fittest rules. She highlights the "tender interactions" among creatures who thrive through cooperation and explains how these serve as a model for Christian community. Her message is convincing—we need each other. Yet I have one hesitation. Ruth Bancewicz writes, "The deadly marine wonder, the Portuguese man o' war, resembles a jellyfish with its beautiful blue and purple ship-shaped bladder and impressive 30-foot stinging tentacles. What may at first appear to be a single organism is actually a colony of four completely different types of polyp."[3] They work so closely together that they appear to be one organism. Is this the aim of Christian community? Should people observe us as one body where neither the foot nor the eye is recognizable? This is not what Paul is saying.

Christian community is not uniformity where we reduce what makes us distinct in order to make us one. Such communities exert pressure on people to conform to one way of thinking or follow a prescribed way to live as a Christian. The miracle of Christian community is learning to live in unity amid our diversity where Christ's real activity through the Spirit enables us to overcome the dividing walls between us. Mutuality in a Christian community involves people figuring out how their differences are beneficial to one another as much as what they have in common. Easy to say. As we all know from experience, this is rather difficult to do.

Theologian Jeremy Begbie is at my college to give a lecture. He plays a *C* on the piano and asks if this is God's intent for Christian community. Does God intend for our unity to carry the same tone? Next, he plays a beautiful, complex cord and claims this as a better vision for us because each distinct note is essential for the robust sound. A recent Android commercial called "Monotone" makes a similar claim by stringing a piano so that all eighty-eight notes play the same sound. The young pianist plays a complicated piece, but the sound is flat. He then turns to a normal piano behind him, and the rich combination of tones echoes from the keys. Android's tagline appears: "be together. not the same." This pluralist claim is powerful and important because it resists blurring differences to achieve unity much like the new Portuguese man o' war organism eclipsing the distinctiveness of four organisms. Yet it misses one important piece.

We have to work very hard to create a beautiful, rich sound. Celebrating differences alone will create a cacophony, not a melody, and lead to extreme individualism. The church has a unique calling. Melodious unity requires actually becoming interdependent where we work hard to seize our differences for mutually beneficial

> **Celebrating differences alone will create a cacophony, not a melody, and lead to extreme individualism.**

relationships that ultimately testify to God's presence among us. Remember that the Spirit is our source of power who makes the impossible possible.

MUTUALITY'S TELOS

The mutualistic relationship shared by the oxpecker and rhino illustrate our interdependence. I need you, and you need me because we are in this together. However, this analogy is also limited. Each does benefit from having the other around based on the exchange of resources—food, health, and safety. The relationship is transactional. For Christian communities, this can be equated with my characterization of a supportive relationship between a Christian and the church. If our interactions merely add up to the exchange of resources that benefit my faith, I reduce you to a tool for my spiritual life. Yes, the church and other Christians should support a person's faith. But this is only a partial truth and like my daughter's galloping-mare version of a seahorse. *I* am not the end. God and God's purpose are always the focus of this story.

God is raising a people who act as a sign pointing to the glory of God and future reign where people live in right relationship with God and others. Valuing mutuality as a community should stimulate personal transformation to build the body as we rub shoulders with each other. We move from a focus on ourselves to our ability to live in unity as a reciprocal church. This echoes Jesus' prayer for the church: "I have given them the glory that you gave me, that they may be one as we are one—I in them and you in me—so that they may be brought to complete unity. Then the world will know that you sent me and have loved them even as you have loved me" (John 17:22-23).

Since Christ generates and maintains Christian community through the Spirit, valuing mutuality means embracing our interdependence—giving special attention rather than eclipsing our differences—as an avenue for personal transformation and growth toward unity as a sign of God's redemptive movement. How might mutuality become a driving value in our communities? First, we have to overcome an obstacle in our churches specific to young people.

SUPPORTING ADOLESCENT DEVELOPMENT

Impeding mutuality. The blaring sound of sirens at 2 a.m. is never a good sign. In our little New Hampshire town, a man's home burns to the ground before the firefighters can gain control of the flames. The homeowner and his dog survive but suffer extensive burns. Down the street lives a ten-year-old boy whose compassion prompts him to act. He sets up a lemonade stand with a simple sign that reads "Help Mr. Evans." News spreads quickly, and in two days he raises thousands of dollars. In the following weeks, the town recognizes him as a hero and model for others. His leadership and initiative are impressive for sure. Did you also notice that this kid breaks out of his typical role? He is supposed to be a *receiver* of all the good things adults want to *pass* to him and not a leader in the community. Maybe rather than calling him a hero, we should call him a rebel.

Earlier we examined how language functions. In a service-based culture, phrases such as "passing on the faith" take on meaning and perpetuate two roles: the passer (adults) and the receiver (kids). This one-way relationship flow stems from our deep love and care for young people. It is right and good that we want to pass faith to them, and yes the community does bear this responsibility. Yet restricting the relationship flow to just one direction endangers the whole community by resisting the mutual flow of relationship, which is an avenue for transformation. Our fear for young people, even when warranted, can intensify this. The one-way relationship flow, where adults "pass faith" to kids, might be of good intention but actually impedes their growth as well as the community's. Do we benefit from having youth around just as we assume youth benefit from adults? Here's another consideration: when a community values mutuality, we provide what is critical to a young person's development.

Theories supporting adolescent development have undergone two significant changes in the last three decades. We already explored the first change. Adolescents face not one but two developmental tasks: *who I am* (independence) and *who I am with others* (interdependence). If we relate this loosely to Christian identity, young people are discovering *who I am in Christ* and *who I am with others in the Christian community*. I own a T-shirt from a youth ministry event that declares in bold letters "Own Your Faith." From a developmental perspective, this sounds similar to the earlier definition of identity formation as only independence. Maybe I should get a sharpie and add interdependence by writing, "Own Your Faith *with Us*."

Reciprocity and human development. A second insight into adolescent development focuses on the interdependent relationship between young people and the environments they live in, such as family, churches, and schools. Two terms deserve our attention: *reciprocity* and *relative plasticity*.

Reciprocity. Throughout the 1900s, developmental researchers generally agreed that human development is a product of the interactions between people and their environments. Yet the manner in which they conducted this research paid more attention to either the person or the environments rather than the *process between them*. In 1998, Urie Bronfenbrenner proposed a new theoretical model claiming that human development occurs in the midst of the interactions a person has with family, peers, schools, and institutions.[4] This should sound a bit like my definition of reciprocation in the introduction. It's the push and pull, back and forth motion between people that needs our attention.

A person and their environments are mutually influential. This idea finds its roots in the classic nature-nurture debate.[5] Researchers who study development have long thought that both nature (biological hardwiring) and nurture (environment) influence a person's development. The nature-nurture debate centers on which has weightier influence or greater force in human development. Bronfenbrenner's use of the term *reciprocity* affirms that both the person and the environments exert influence on one another. For example, the church affects Eduardo even as Eduardo influences the church. Think of this like a bidirectional arrow: person ↔ environments. Reciprocity does not claim that all influence is equal but does assert that there is a two-way flow. Both Eduardo and the church exert influence on the other even as there are, as Bronfenbrenner says, "degrees of reciprocity in the exchange."[6] What should we conclude? Mutuality is central to the developmental process.

Bronfenbrenner argues that the greatest potential for positive development exists when the person and the environments in which they live adapt to each other. This requires interactions that occur regularly, take advantage of reciprocity, and endure over time.[7] The technical term for this adaptation is *plasticity*, which means that both the person and environment have the capacity to change or adapt based on the other's influence.

Developmental researcher Richard Lerner characterizes this potential for change as "relative plasticity." Changes are *relative* since both person and environments have constraints.[8] For example, a person may have social anxiety and therefore limit their engagement with a community. Or a community may have limited resources to offer the person. Relative plasticity highlights how the person and the environments are acting and adapting to the other with their present abilities, knowledge, and resources. Clearly all person ↔ environment adaptations will be contextual since we are speaking about real persons living in real places and communities. Yet researchers search for optimal conditions that foster healthy development for young people and communities. For one of these conditions, let's turn to research on mentoring relationships.

Relational processes. In 2006, developmental researcher Rene Spencer published groundbreaking research conducted through Big Brothers Big Sisters organizations. Spencer addressed the growing concern that mentor relationships are not as effective in promoting positive development as anticipated. She established a theoretical base for mentoring research that focused on relational process versus the traditional measurements on youth outcomes (e.g., increased school performance, avoiding high risk behaviors). Drawing from relational theory, she examined the connection between "psychological health and vitality with participation in growth-fostering relationship."[9] Spencer interviewed twenty-four pairs of successful adolescent-adult mentoring relationships to learn about their relational processes. Of the twenty-four pairs, all but one self-reported experiencing the following four relational qualities:

- *Authenticity*: They perceive their interactions as genuine. They give each other access to honest thoughts, feelings, and intentions, and experience the other as engaged and responsive.

- *Empathy*: They understand each other's "frame of reference" and "affective experience." They perceive the other as emotionally responsive because each tries to see and feel as the other person does. They recognize the complexity of their lives rather than just one aspect.

- *Collaboration*: They actively work toward a goal together, and both feel like a valued participant even if one is more skilled than the other.

- *Companionship*: They spend time together, and during hard times they perceive that someone believes in them.

Authenticity leads to feeling we share life. Empathy leads to feeling we understand each other. Collaboration leads to feeling committed to one another. Companionship leads to feeling valued.

Based on these research findings, we can reflect on three insights: (1) Adolescent development involves a person's evolving relationship with self and others; (2) the greatest potential for positive development exists when the person and the environments adapt to each other; and (3) When interactions include feeling loved and valued, mentor relationships foster healthy development.

These insights should push us to examine the one-way-relationship flow between adults and young people in the church. This relationship pattern likely impedes a young person's development as well as the community's growth. We already believe adults and communities can influence young people. Do we also think youth are actors in their own faith formation and, maybe more difficult to consider, do we perceive young people to be actors who influence our church? Remember that God created each of us to actively join God's redemptive purposes. The New Testament pages repeatedly affirm that relationships are a primary avenue for our personal and communal transformation. If it is also true that human development includes reciprocal influences, person ↔ environments, then valuing mutuality should permeate our communities, which leaves young people feeling loved and valued. What does this look like? What forms might this take in your church? *A reciprocal church values mutuality and makes giving and receiving a central practice in its community's life.*

MUTUALITY IN ACTION

Sharing faith. Over thirty years ago, pastor and theologian John Westerhoff criticized the way churches taught the Christian faith. He claimed the reason churches were not producing faithful Christians was because teaching overfocused on the content of faith. Westerhoff sought to cast a different vision for sharing faith that overlaps with what I am calling mutuality. He writes, "To be a Christian is to ask: What can I bring another? Not: What do I want that person to know or be? It means being open to learn from another person (even a child) as well as to share one's understandings and ways."[10] Adults should share the faith while at the same time anticipate having faith shared with them.

Miroslav Volf's description of the shared nature of faith adds further clarity when he defines confessing faith (meaning confessing faith in Christ, not confessing sins).[11] He argues that confessing faith is *performative* because it is an action carried out *by* a person *with* the community. When a community joins together in fellowship to do things such as sing, listen to Scripture, bring offerings, and receive the sacraments, they are confessing faith together. This objective performance with others must be accompanied by a person's subjective faith. This is why confession in a community "takes place *between* persons" where "I am both communicating something to them and inviting them into something."[12] There is potential for each person to give to the community and to receive from the community. For Volf, this is a shared act where "the confession of faith of one person leads to that of others."[13] Faith is both received *through* the community and claimed independently by the person. Confessing faith both constitutes and sustains the church.[14]

This is a familiar experience. When we hear someone confess faith through a song, a spontaneous prayer, or reciting a creed, this encourages our faith. As a result, our own confession strengthens. Shared confession is likely one reason why the Hillsong concerts, concerts of prayer, and large youth events are such powerful experiences. Hearing others confess faith elicits faith in us and prompts us to join the confession more boldly. This is what Volf means by *giving and receiving* faith.

There are times in my life when I walk into the community of faith discouraged or full of doubts. In these moments, I need the community's faith to empower and encourage me. Likewise, I also find myself telling friends and young people who describe their faith as weak or unsure that I will have faith for them. By saying this, I do not claim to replace their personal commitment but to stand with them during a vulnerable time. I am acknowledging the ebb and flow of faith in real life and demonstrating that we are in this together. All of us have moments when we stand with the centurion and proclaim to Christ, "I do believe; help me overcome my unbelief!" (Mark 9:24).

Sharing faith means we benefit from having one another around. Receiving faith empowers us to persevere while giving faith guards against the tendency for *me* to be the subject of faith. When this happens, we become interdependent. In addition, this is not just a transaction between us like the oxpecker and rhino. Becoming interdependent is what it means to live in unity and demonstrates Christ's reconciling activity among us. Religious educator John Westerhoff captures this, saying, "We are corporate selves who live in a continual dynamic relationship with all others and with God."[15]

Sharing responsibility. Many of our models for relationships are top-down: The older cares for the younger, the wise helps the immature, the teacher educates the student, and the parent raises the child. A mentor becomes a verb who mentors a mentee. Yet if a community expresses mutuality by sharing faith, responsibility must also be shared. Similar to the definition of *reciprocity*, there are varying degrees of exchange between the person and community. Sharing responsibility for one another's faith will often mean people carry different loads. Carrying a smaller portion remains as critical as a larger amount when we genuinely share responsibility.

Appropriate roles still exist when we share responsibility for one another's faith. My world is rocked by the diagnosis that my mom has lung cancer. The tumor is operable, and she prepares to have a portion of her lung removed. My kids adore their Mimi, and I know the news rattles them too. I anticipate their first question but do not have an answer prepared. "Will Mimi be okay?" Without thinking, I quickly put my hand out in front of them with my palm facing the ceiling and say, "Imagine this is God's hand, and Mimi is lying right in the middle of it. God holds her for us." Through a series of tragic circumstances, we lose my mom. For months, the pain of grief and death's finality overwhelm me. I find it difficult to carry out the most basic daily tasks.

In my darkest moments, Annie, who is seven, is at my side with hand outstretched and her palm facing the ceiling. No words are needed. I receive the strength I need. Our roles remain the same. I am the mother, and she is my daughter. I am still teaching Annie how to pray even as her prayer offering penetrates the depth of my aching soul. We are in this together and share responsibility for one another.

Sharing responsibility means that each of us needs to reflect on how our actions impact others. New Testament scholar James Howard's interpretation of Ephesians helps us picture this. Throughout the book, Paul impresses on the Ephesians the need to maintain unity. Chapter four opens with an admonition outlining the actions required for living "a life worthy" (Ephesians 4:1). The list calls people to reflect on their actions: "Be completely humble and gentle; be patient, bearing with one another in love" (v. 2). Paul compares and contrasts the impact of their actions in verses 25-32. Each should "*put off falsehood*" and "*speak truthfully* to your neighbor, for we are all members of one body" (italics added). These early Christians should refrain from "unwholesome talk" and speak to "benefit those who listen." Anyone who steals must instead work so "they may have something to share with those in need." Actions with a detrimental impact such as "bitterness, rage and anger, brawling and slander, along with every form of malice" should be replaced with kindness, compassion, and forgiveness. Each person is ultimately responsible for making a positive impact on others. Paul explains, "From him the whole body, joined and held together by every supporting ligament, grows and builds itself up in love, *as each part does its work*" (v. 16; italics added). We all share responsibility for one another's faith as we work toward unity, and we express this responsibility when we weigh the impact of our actions on one another.

Sharing love. A community of faith who shares faith and responsibility values mutuality and welcomes our interdependence. Place this alongside the insights from adolescent development. Giving and receiving faith acknowledges a young person's evolving relationship with both self and others. Faith strengthens as we all own faith with others. As the community confesses faith in Christ, the person and community affect each other's confession. Sharing responsibility for one another's faith can foster healthy development as young people and the church appropriate faith together. When we practice giving and receiving faith, our interdependence is real.

Mutuality cannot be produced. It can only be demonstrated. Demonstrating love is central to the gospel, and therefore love is mutuality's foundation. Read Ephesians 4:16 again and note that love is the catalyst for building the body: "From him the whole body, joined and held together by every supporting ligament, grows and builds itself up *in love*, as each part does its work" (italics added). Love is at the core of Jesus' description of the law, "You shall not murder," in Matthew 5. His audience knew the law and followed the law but forgot the intent of the law. "You shall not murder" has broader implications. Jesus calls his disciples to prioritize reconciliation with their brothers or sisters before bringing gifts to the altar. In Howard's words, Jesus "reoriented the law around the love commands and reemphasized the community aspect of the law."[16] The aim here is more than accurately interpreting the law. Jesus calls his followers to demonstrate love to one another.

Living interdependently requires rubbing shoulders with one another over an extended period of time. We learn how to give faith and receive faith. Taking responsibility for our impact on one another is a never-ending process. In the midst of this, opportunities to demonstrate love will occur at every turn.

Mutuality cannot be produced. It can only be demonstrated.

Recall the relational processes that support healthy mentoring relationships. Loving by sharing faith will express *authenticity* and *empathy*. Loving by sharing responsibility will involve *collaboration* and *companionship*. These demonstrations of love hold the possibility that young people will experience adults who share life's journey with them, understand them, commit to them, and deeply value them. *And* vice versa.

The 2006 film *Akeelah and the Bee* captures the power that demonstrating love can have in a community. Eleven-year-old Akeelah lives in a poor and often violent neighborhood in Los Angeles. Her mom works multiple jobs to provide further opportunities for her kids. The principal of Akeelah's school comes up with a plan to stop the school's downward spiral by getting kids involved in the spelling bee. Akeelah loves letters and words, which makes her the perfect candidate. Throughout the movie, we watch Akeelah struggle to receive help. She has learned to be guarded simply from trying to survive in her rough neighborhood. People in her life also struggle to give her the help she needs. Her brother fights the pull toward gang life; her spelling coach's grief makes him withdraw from life; her mom's financial pressure results in a lack of time and a struggle to trust the school; her best friend just wants guys to notice her. Yet Akeelah keeps winning spelling bees.

Despite all odds, Akeelah stands on the stage at the National Spelling Bee. If she spells the final word correctly, she will be a champion. The word caller says, "Spell the word *pulchritude*." Her face brightens and eyes close—she knows the word. As she says each letter, her memory fills with people in her life who helped prepare her for this moment. It is no longer just Akeelah spelling the word. Across the screen flash the people in her life saying each letter with her: her brother, a gang member, her best friend, the principal, her coach, and, of course, her mom. *Pulchritude* means beautiful, and when this troubled community learns to give and receive, the result is beautiful.

Since Christ generates and maintains Christian community through the Spirit, valuing mutuality means embracing our interdependence—giving special attention to our differences—as an avenue for personal transformation and growth toward unity. If we practice giving and receiving faith, we can become a beautiful sign of God's redemptive movement. We are in this together.

8

SEEING BEYOND THE EPIDEMIC

RECOGNIZING POTENTIAL

STRUGGLE **DEFINES L**YDIA**'**S **LIFE**. Her home situation is messy with a domineering parent and a sibling with significant health issues. Neither money nor free time is a family asset. Lydia gravitates toward kids who get into trouble. On a youth group trip, friends cajole her into stealing candy during a pit stop at a convenience store. Somehow, she always seems to be in the damaged room when we check out at camp. Every time I see Lydia, there is some unfolding drama in her life. She does not come to me seeking advice or even solace. The only thing she wants is affirmation that everyone and everything is terrible. If I do not sing this negative song, she continues to elaborate on details and raises the shock level until I exclaim, "That's awful." Admittedly, when Lydia walks in, I see a problem.

Joel looks different to me. He too comes from a rough home situation. His dad leaves when he is ten. While other kids his age play video games and run around with friends, he takes care of younger siblings. He's had a job since age fourteen to help his mom pay the bills. I never hear Joel complain or speak resentfully about his circumstances. He seems to embrace life as it is. At Bible studies, he asks thoughtful questions that serve as a catalyst for great group discussions. Joel wants to know Jesus and takes every opportunity to invite others to do the same. When I see Joel, I see great potential.

Different stories, different responses. In one I see a problem and in another I see potential. Today, Joel is well-rounded and expresses a passionate faith. Lydia's life remains unstable, and faith lives somewhere in the shadows. Yet I wonder about my contribution to their outcomes. What could I have done differently? Is it possible that the problem lens through which I saw Lydia adversely influenced her? If I had adjusted my vision to look for Lydia's potential, would the outcome be different?

Let's backtrack one more step before answering these questions. Is it only a person's actions and attitude that determine when we see problem or potential? Or is there more at work? When we see a young person, what shapes the lens we see through? I fear we are more disposed to one lens than another.

TEENAGERS: AN EPIDEMIC

My son and I are driving down our street when a blue Volkswagen cuts the corner too tightly and barely misses us as I slam on the brakes. My son exclaims, "Teenage drivers!" Bewildered, I look over at Mason and inquire, "Did you see the driver?" "No," he replies, "but that's how teenagers drive." I did see the driver.

Problematizing young people is in our society's DNA.

He is a kind old man who lives around the corner, and apparently he likes to imagine himself as a NASCAR driver. Mason's assumption that this was a teenage driver is telling. Problematizing young people is in our society's DNA.

If you start scanning articles about teenagers, you will soon discover a narrative that claims we face *an epidemic*.

- "Teens Know They Are Addicted to Smartphones"—*U.S. News and World Report*, May 2016

- "There Is No Stopping Teenagers from Sharing Naked Selfies" —*Economic Times*, October 2014

- "Fewer US Teens Smoking, But Smoke Problem Persists" —*CBS News*, January 2016

- "The Collateral Damage of a Teenager: What Adolescence Does to Adolescents Is Nowhere Near as Brutal as What It Does to Their Parents"—*New York Magazine*, January 2014

- "23m Adolescents at Risk of Unintended Pregnancy"—*Daily Star*, May 2016

- "Why Teenagers Hit Puberty and Take Dumb Risks"—*The Atlantic*, June 2015

- "Teenager Drivers? Be Very Afraid"—*New York Times*, March 2016

Chris Elliott, writer for British newspaper *The Guardian*, summarizes the scene well: "If you are reading a story in the newspapers about 13- to 19-year-olds there is a fair chance it will be about homelessness, violent deaths, cyber-bullying or teenage pregnancy."[1] Sometimes the content beneath such headlines may temper the epidemic narrative. For example, the author of a 2012 *Wall Street Journal* article challenges the portrayal of recent MRI research, saying, "Brain research is often taken to mean that adolescents are really just defective adults—grown-ups with a missing part."[2] The article insightfully interprets the current research on adolescent brain development. Yet the wording of the title "What's Wrong with the Teenage Mind?" grabs our attention by feeding the epidemic narrative.

We are not the first adults to problematize teenagers. In fact, this story line parallels the emergence of adolescence as a sociological category in the early 1900s. In 1904, psychologist G. Stanley Hall wrote the inaugurating volumes on adolescent development. Hall describes adolescents as moving out of their "beast-like impulses" to being civilized. He portrays normal adolescent development as a time of "storm and stress."[3] Hall's connections between adolescence, stress, and overcoming shortfalls were extremely influential over the next century.[4] In the 1960s, we see it in Erik Erikson's description of adolescents needing to resolve the *identity crisis*.[5] Developmental psychologist Richard Lerner says this "deficit language" creates a vision of adolescents who are "at risk" to themselves and others.[6] Mark Twain's infamous words say it best: "When a boy turns thirteen, put him in a barrel and feed him through a knot hole. When he turns sixteen, plug up the hole."

According to Learner, "uncivilized behavior" is the story line we believe.[7] Our response is to create an action plan. Organizations, parents, and churches work hard to protect young people and help them overcome their deficiencies. We develop intervention programs, health campaigns, and education plans to supplement teenage shortfalls. Researchers perpetuate the stigma by measuring successful development through the *nots*—not using drugs or alcohol, not dropping out of school, or not getting pregnant.[8] As I describe earlier, add to this the mass media's depiction of teenagers as haphazard, broken, problems to be managed, and even potentially dangerous to themselves and others. In this narrative, adolescence in American culture is something we fear. This fear drives schools, parents, and churches alike. Maybe there is an epidemic. Maybe we need to download the latest version of the book telling us how to survive the teenage years or take Mark Twain's advice and buy a barrel.

As you can imagine, this story line also influences young people's impression of themselves and their peers such as Mason's conclusion that the bad driver must be a teenager. The story line also shapes how adults view young people. In a 2015 study conducted by Search Institute, researchers demonstrate how adult outlook influences behavior toward young people.[9] When adults focus on a young person's limitations, expectations lower, learning options are fewer, less time is spent together, and conversation drops to a minimum. It saddens me to look back and see this in my relationship with Lydia. Looking at teenagers through a problem lens can be detrimental.

Maybe teenagers themselves are not the epidemic. Maybe the epidemic is bound to what we see. Adolescent development researchers are making a dramatic turn in the field of positive youth development (PYD). For example, William Damon describes the adolescent developmental task not to overcome deficits and risks but to "explore the world, gain competence, and acquire the capacity to contribute importantly to the world." Instead of diagnosing and treating youth's "maladaptive tendencies," adults should be "engaging them in productive activities."[10] PYD researcher Peter Benson reorients our vision by describing young people as invaluable resources for society.[11] As he says in a 2011 TEDx Talk, "Youth are not vessels to be filled but fires to be lit."[12]

This page in history is turning. I join with many others who are working to change the epidemic story line. The first step requires that we, adults committed to young people, reflect on what we presently see. *Beyond the specific actions or attitudes of the person*, are young people in your church or ministry viewed as a problem to fix or as potential to unveil? Is your approach to youth ministry primarily geared toward helping young people overcome deficiencies or unleash potential? Is the *potential* lens or the *problem* lens driving your teaching, programs, and decisions? Both lenses are likely present, but does one persist over the other?

YOUTH MINISTRY: THE PROBLEM LENS

Based on my experience and research, the problem lens is more common in youth ministries for three reasons. First, the epidemic narrative is alive and well in Christian communities. We fear for the well-being of young people. This fear looms in the minds of parents, pastors, boards, and likely you and me. The world is scary. Whether or not young people face more dangers in comparison to past generations is debatable. But one feature does make the time we live in distinct: due to unprecedented access to large amounts of information, we are increasingly *aware* of dangers. The sirens reverberate through our social media newsfeeds and conversa-

We act like they have a deficit— faith—and we need to help them overcome this shortfall.

tions. All of us want to protect kids, and this is right and good. I laugh every time I see Blue Cross Blue Shield's ad with the kid wrapped in thick layers of bubble wrap. That is exactly what we want to do. Still, one consequence of our information-accessible world is that it can magnify and amplify the fear and the danger. The problem lens intensifies as we seek to protect young people from both real and perceived danger.

Second, Christians have an additional layer of fear beyond safety and well-being. We fear young people will not continue to follow Jesus. In part, such fear motivated this book and others like it. Research indicates that rising generations are increasingly walking away from the church. In a 2018 report, Barna finds that among those born between 1999 and 2015 the number of young people who identify as atheist doubles that of the current adult population.[13] Because teaching the faith is our responsibility, such reports require a response. Often our reactions include repeatedly going back to Bible basics or stressing moral teachings. We hope that right knowledge will secure faith and wrap young people in protective bubble wrap. When our teachings, programs, and conversations focus on ensuring a teenager's lifelong faith, we demonstrate that the problem lens is alive and well. We act like they have a deficit—faith—and we need to help them overcome this shortfall.

Third, our *amazement* reactions to young people solidify my conviction that the problem lens is widespread. When young people, and kids of any age, do something great, we stand back and marvel as if we have seen a miracle. Many years ago my church had a tradition of inviting high school seniors to preach a brief sermon to the congregation. Seats were at a premium on these Sundays. With tears of pride flowing, adult after adult walked up to these students in amazement. It was simply baffling that such wisdom and teaching could come from these kids. Why such surprise? Because it is not what we expect to see from these deficient human beings. I bet you have heard countless adult volunteers declare their wonder at how much they gain from working with young people. This will always be the case when we arrive on the scene ready to help with the deficit, but unaware that they will positively affect us.

I see this in myself. We have our eight-year-old daughter with us at a weekend youth retreat. From among the seminar offerings, she picks one about sharing your faith. At first I thought this was odd and, if honest, a poor choice. She should go to something to help her learn more about how to read the Bible. My jaw drops as she compassionately explains how many of her friends do not go to church or know about God. Why am I so surprised about her desire to share her faith? My vision for her potential is suffocating beneath my fear that she might not end up with a solid faith.

If our predominant lens for young people is problem-centered, there will be negative implications. We will be prone to focus on the objectives we have for them similar to approaching a project. Our job will be to fix, to tell, and to give. In Brazilian educator Paulo Freire's words, we reduce them to "empty receptacles" that need to be filled.[14] Young people will become receivers of the faith, and it will be our responsibility to secure their salvation for them. This *fixing* posture increases the growing chasm between adults and young people. Practical theologian Chap Clark captures this when he describes teenagers living in "the world beneath" where parents busily provide opportunities for their kids, but kids ironically experience their parents as absent.[15] Nel Noddings, an educational philosopher, describes this same phenomenon in education where teachers work on behalf of students without students feeling "cared for."[16] Are youth ministries perpetuating the same adult-teenager divide by reducing young people to being problems to fix?

You might find yourself arguing with me at this point. Even if your head is nodding because you agree that seeing young people through the problem lens alone is detrimental, is the potential lens and turning a blind eye to the real dangers facing young people the answer? No, this would be equally problematic.

Wendy Mogel writes a series of parenting books in which she weaves together her knowledge and experience as a clinical psychologist with the Jewish teaching of her faith tradition.[17] She focuses on developing resilience, an essential character trait young people need in life. In her first book, titled *The Blessing of the Skinned Knee*, one of the main problems she sees facing young people today is their unwavering confidence in how "preternaturally [beyond what is normal] important they were to their parents."[18] They feel valued too much by us? And to the degree that it is detrimental to their well-being? I can make my kids feel like they are too special to me? Well—yes. If my kids experience themselves as insurmountably important, they misconstrue the ordering of the world, think they are the center of it, and develop a sense of entitlement. As I define the potential lens, it is not the antithesis of the problem lens where we only speak of a young person's greatness without recognizing needs for growth, knowledge, correction, discipline, and experience. Without these, young people may well experience our care for them preternaturally.

The potential lens sees the complex makeup of a young person and works to keep the wider vision in the forefront. The 2004 movie *National Treasure*, starring Nicholas Cage as Benjamin Franklin Gates, illustrates this well. For generations, Ben's family has hunted for a war chest hidden after the Revolutionary War by the Founding Fathers. Ben and his friends take up the hunt. In the midst of following a set of clues, they discover Ben Franklin's glasses. These glasses have numerous lenses of different colors and views. Like a decoding pin, flipping the lens around changes what they see. They need to find the right order of lenses to read the clue. In the same way, there are multiple lenses at work when we see young people. I am not saying that we need to choose the potential lens and ignore the problem lens. Instead, we need to flip through our ordering of the lenses to see more clearly. In our current situation the problem lens is dominating and blurring our ability to see the potential young people have to contribute to God's movement among us.

In our current situation the problem lens is dominating and blurring our ability to see the potential young people have to contribute to God's movement among us.

SEEING POTENTIAL: ADJUSTING THE LENSES

Seeing potential in young people stems from our shared identity as a people belonging to God. *We* are a people brought together for God's purposes. In everyday life, our *we* identity takes form when we covenant to join a local church and contribute to the community's mission. If we see young people as deficient or having some deficit needing to be added on to them (the problem lens), we undermine God's good creation. Seeing potential in young people begins with two declarations about God: God is both Creator and Redeemer.

Creator. Acknowledging God as Creator might include marveling over creation's magnificence like a California sunset or a breathtaking view from atop Montana's mountain crests. Yet even more than this, to proclaim God is Creator *turns our attention toward God* as the author of life. As theologian Stanley Grenz describes, our lives are "derived." God bestows existence like a gracious gift that we receive. It follows then that creation belongs to and is dependent on its Creator. We read this emphasis in Acts 17:28: "In him we move and have our being." Young people are created beings. They cannot choose to come into existence or flourish apart from their Creator. Seeing a young person's potential is first an act of worship offered to the Creator.

Additionally, what God creates brings honor and glory to God. Early Christian writers fought against the dominant dualistic influence in Greek thought that viewed the material world as evil and the spiritual world as good. In the midst of this, the church persistently proclaimed God as Creator in worship.[19] This is why early confessions like the Apostles' and Nicene Creeds declare God to be

Seeing a young person's potential is first an act of worship offered to the Creator.

"maker of heaven and earth." This phrase intentionally emphasized the goodness of God's creation and set Christianity apart from the predominant view of their day. What God creates—this world, our bodies, and all of life—has inherent value to our Creator. Far from being deficient or having a deficit-based humanity, young people are created beings who bring honor and glory to God.

Looking for potential in young people draws our attention to their Creator to whom we attribute praise because each one is a valuable part of creation. This lens recognizes all existence as bestowed, and as a created being a person's potential is always God dependent. God creates young people to flourish in relationship with God, self, others, and all of creation for God's glory. Looking for this potential is an act of worship.

Creator-Redeemer. Seeing potential also takes into account the magnitude of sin. Recall Bonhoeffer's definition of sin as its consequences on relationships. Sin results in lost potential to flourish in relationship with God, self, others, and creation. The good news is that God is also Redeemer. We worship the author of creation who bestows life and *continues* to redeem all things amid our brokenness. Bonhoeffer describes this as God's present activity in Christ, who died and rose from the dead and continues to come daily to renew us again and again. Right now, through the Spirit, Christ is doing for us what we cannot do for ourselves. Christ is presently advocating for us as a *priest* making intercession, as a *prophet* proclaiming liberation, and as a *king* reigning for all eternity.

Young people need the Creator-Redeemer's intervention to release them from sin's power. The brokenness, fear, pain, rebellion, impulsivity, and carelessness of young people are real. Just like adults, young people look for salvation in today's dominant cultural narratives based on fame and wealth rather than in their Creator-Redeemer. Young people desperately need Jesus as they swim in a consumable world that offers temporary highs from purchasing stuff, achieving the next video game level, gaining social status, creating a social media identity, and wearing the right label. Jesus responds to these parched-lipped kids just as he reaches out to the woman at the well: "Everyone who drinks this water will be thirsty again, but whoever drinks the water I give them will never thirst. Indeed, the water I give them will become in them a spring of water welling up to eternal life" (John 4:13-14). Jesus seeks young people like a good shepherd in care of his sheep, saying, "I have come that they may have life, and have it to the full" (John 10:10). In this sense, Jesus did not come to be a problem fixer; rather, he came to set young people free for God.

How does the word *for* strike you in the previous sentence? This is the central aspect of the potential lens—to be free *for* God. Practical theologian Thomas H. Groome rightly criticizes our descriptions of Christ's work that only emphasize saving us *from* our sins and leave out what we are saved *for*.[20] We seem to miss the essential second piece. If we are freed *from* our sins, what are we freed *for*? God is Creator-Redeemer, and we are created and redeemed to be free *for* God. Sin does bind and restrict us from being free *for* God because we want to be free for ourselves. Therefore, Jesus' self-sacrificing gift sets us free *from* our sins so we have freedom *for* our Creator. Christ's life, death, and resurrection releases us *from* sin's power so we might be free *for* God and God's purposes. If we only focus on Christ saving us *from* our sins, this keeps us gazing backward. Christ invites us to look forward at what God creates and redeems us *for*.

Paulea has a thirteen-year-old daughter named Shanna. Shanna knows the family's commitment to go to church every Sunday, yet she increasingly resists going. Shanna is making Sunday mornings pretty miserable for everyone. On this particular Sunday, she continues this behavior during the worship service by teasing her brother, mocking her sister, and making it impossible for anyone in the family, and everyone around her, to pay attention. Paulea is done. She whispers, "Get out of your seat. We are leaving." Shanna stubbornly crosses her arms, for surely her mom is only threatening. Paulea then hisses, "Stand up." Shanna gets nervous and does not want others to notice the scene, so she starts promising to behave. Through clenched teeth, Paulea turns on the don't-mess-with-your-mother-tone and demands, *"Get up and go to the car."* Shanna complies.

Doors slam, and Shanna's remorseful words start flowing. Paulea ignores her and starts driving, which only increases Shanna's anxiety. "Where are we going? I'm sorry. I won't do it again."

Paulea grabs a pad of paper and pen and tosses them at Shanna. She orders, "Make a list of everything you've done wrong this morning and all the people you've hurt in the wake of your poor behavior."

Shanna quickly responds, "Okay, I'll do it, Mom, just tell me where we are going."

Unmoved, Paulea continues, "Now make a second list, and write down who God wants you to be."

Shanna busily follows these orders all the while pleading to know where they are going. The car stops at Starbucks. This makes no sense to Shanna who is becoming rather contrite at this point, and she whimpers, "I don't deserve Starbucks. Why are we here?" Paulea agrees with her and tells her to get out of the car, go up to the counter, and order whatever she wants. Shanna meekly orders her favorite Frappuccino.

"You're hungry, aren't you? Order food too," directs Paulea.

Sitting at a corner table, Shanna nervously plays with her lists. "Lay the papers between us," Paulea says softly.

The feast arrives, and both Shanna and Paulea start to cry. Shanna chokes out, "I'm sorry, Mom, I don't deserve this."

Paulea talks through the first list and agrees that she did all of this plus a few more things that she writes down. Then, Paulea moves on to the second list. Shanna has written that God wants her to be respectful, kind, generous, and loving. Paulea again agrees and also writes down some of Shanna's specific gifts: compassionate, intelligent, athletic, and visional. Paulea brings it all together, saying, "You're right, Shanna. You don't deserve Starbucks right now. I have you here because I want you to see the contrast between your behavior today and what God wants for you. Shanna, God wants to set you free to be the person on the second list." Paulea rips up the morning behavior list with tears spilling down her tired face, and explains, "With every sip you take of that Frappuccino, let the good taste remind you that God wants more for you—more than you can even want for yourself. You are God's valuable creation. Just like I tore up the list of your guilt, Christ destroys sin's power in your life. Why? To set you free to be the person on the second list. Jesus died for you, Shanna, not to make you compliant or wallow in your unworthiness. God created you with a potential for God beyond what you can imagine. I see a glimpse of what is on the second list already. Jesus died to save you *from* your sins so that you can be free *for* God."

On her own, Shanna takes the second list home and tacks it to the wall beside her bed. Because frustrated Paulea took on the practice of looking through the potential lens, Shanna also caught a glimpse of this vision. God is her Creator-Redeemer, and as a valuable created being, Christ through the Spirit saves her *from* the power of sin to unleash her created potential to be free *for* God. The same is true for you, me, and every young person we meet.

9

MOVING BEYOND THE EPIDEMIC

VALUING CONTRIBUTION

W E CAN ADJUST OUR PROBLEM LENS and practice recognizing every young person's potential for God. Yet this does not tell us much about this God-oriented potential. Seeing young people's potential is also bound to humanity's reflection of the *imago Dei* (image of God). Theologians have spilled endless ink over what it means for humanity to reflect the *imago Dei*, and their conclusions generally fall into three groupings. Humans reflect the *imago Dei* in

1. who we are (in our structure), most commonly understood as our rational capacity;

2. what we express (in relationship) with God, others, and creation; and

3. what we do (our function) as God's representatives.

History demonstrates that each view carries its own set of strengths and limitations, and this is the subject of much discussion today. Theologian Marc Cortez is one who argues for building onto the third view (what we do) by emphasizing the future and who we are becoming.[1] Following a growing number of theologians, I will call this the dynamic view.[2]

Using the word *dynamic* resists the *imago Dei* being a static concept like something implanted in us. Especially in the New Testament, the *imago Dei* speaks of "developing toward something."[3] Think of the image of God as our lives representing God in the world. Yet our potential to reflect God with our lives is damaged, restricted, and veiled by sin. Christ saves us *from* our sins, setting us free *for* God. Such freedom increases our capacity to learn to reflect God with our lives. The focus here is on growth and transformation, as Paul describes in 2 Corinthians 3:18: "We all, who with unveiled faces contemplate the Lord's glory, are being transformed *into his image* with ever-increasing glory, which comes from the Lord, who is the Spirit" (italics added). Theologian Daniel Migliore captures Paul's vision of living "into his image" with his future-oriented emphasis, saying, "Being created in the image of God is not a state or condition but a movement with a goal: human beings are restless for a fulfillment of life not yet realized."[4]

Seeing potential in young people begins when we look for and anticipate the dynamic, unfolding transformation in their lives. We often have the privilege of seeing it even before they do. This kind of transformation has form to it. In real time and real life, the Spirit increasingly transforms young people, and us, so that through our lives (in our thoughts, feelings, desires, wills, words, actions, relationships) we might live in ways that represent God's purposes in the world. This means the *imago Dei* calls us to contribute to what God is already doing in the world. Young people have God-created potential to contribute to God's redemptive purposes among us. A reciprocal church values contribution and learns to practice seeing the potential of every young person in its community.

POTENTIAL TO CONTRIBUTE

How does this play out? Do we all need to have dramatic Starbucks heart-to-heart moments with kids, as Paulea did? Although life is full of crucial moments, they cannot be engineered. Valuing contribution needs to reverberate through the community. A study of the word *youth* in the Bible provides a significant

> **A reciprocal church values contribution and learns to practice seeing the potential of every young person in its community.**

insight.[5] It is humorous to notice that both the problem and potential lenses are present in the text. Throughout the Bible, authors repeatedly characterize youth as being prone toward rebellion and unrestrained desire. For example, youthfulness is a metaphor for Israel's disobedience: "You will forget the shame of your youth" (Isaiah 54:4). Youth lack prudence, knowledge, and discretion (Proverbs 1:4). The problem lens is alive and well.

But don't miss the potential lens. There are many references to youthful vigor defined as physical strength and strong health (Job 20:11; 33:25). The eagle is a metaphor for youthful vitality and refers to God's renewal (Psalm 103:5). Even though Timothy as a young church leader receives advice to avoid "the evil desires of youth" (2 Timothy 2:22), Paul also sees his potential with these words of encouragement: "Don't let anyone look down on you because you are young, but set an example for the believers in speech, in conduct, in love, in faith and in purity" (1 Timothy 4:12). In the Bible, youth possess energy, strength, and a life full of possibilities—this is the potential lens. The problem and potential lenses coexist across the text and remind us that both lenses are part of growing up.

There is something else going on with the word *youth* in the Bible that captures my attention: *youth are growing contributors to the community*. Remember my earlier comparison between the Bible's social world and our own? An individualistic social world is widespread in Western societies. We focus on personal growth and individual achievement, such as being on your own, developing yourself, and standing on your own two feet. In contrast, the Bible's collectivist social world values belonging, which a person demonstrates by contributing to the clan. With a collectivist social world in mind, when we encounter *youth* in the Bible, this word designates their evolving relationship with the community rather than only referring to an individual's age bracket (such as ages 12-18).

"Youth" is one of four life phases in the ancient Near East (ANE): childhood, youth, young married (often called maturity), and elder. A person's life phase determines their social ranking in the community, and elders hold the highest status. Compare this to our culture's preoccupation with youthfulness.[6] In the ANE, there would not be a market for anti-aging cream since wrinkles surely emphasize higher status. This means that descriptions of youth (lower status) will be lacking in contrast to the elderly (higher status). A person of higher status is one who contributes significantly to the clan. Consequently, as people move through the life phases, their contribution to the clan is expected to increase. This is true for a child who becomes a youth (generally at the onset of puberty) as well as for a youth who transitions into the maturity life phase once married. Youth are expected to gain knowledge, wisdom, and experience, and move out of their youthful tendencies, so their capacity to contribute to the community increases. Neither getting them ready to make it on their own in the world nor fixing youthful "problems" is the end. In a collectivist society, we can imagine seeing youth as those who have potential for the good of the community.

In individualistic societies, especially when consuming is a condition and community is voluntary, contribution will not likely be a primary value. Instead, we value personal growth. This means churches should *support* a person's faith, and we task youth ministries with securing each young person's faith so they are ready for adulthood. Many have argued this before, using the statement, "Young people aren't the future of the church. They are the church of the present." But young people can only be the church of the present when contribution is a primary value that seeps through programs, mission statements, youth ministry job descriptions, church leaders, and the lens through which adults see young people—potential *for* God as contributors to God's redemptive movement in the world.

CONTRIBUTION VERSUS PARTICIPATION

The phone buzzes with yet another request for the youth to help. I confess that this call and others like it make me grumpy:

- "Wouldn't it be great if the young people served dinner to the seniors?"

- "The kids could set up the chairs in the worship center each week and really contribute to the church."

- "Sharon, would you find a young person to read Scripture during worship once a month?"

Each example is a request for what I will call participation. Participation asks someone to join what is already going on. Participation is important for young people to belong to what is already happening and learn the ways of the community. Yet participation does not always include contribution. Causation is the root of contribution. Valuing contribution asks people *to cause a change* by bringing, adding, creating, endeavoring, improving, or enhancing. Contribution is entrepreneurial at its core. Do we want young people to only join what we are already doing (participation), or do we hope they will also enrich, maybe even change, what we are doing (contribution)?

More than when I was growing up, entrepreneurial contribution is regularly part of a young person's life. My child's first grade writing pages and illustrations are bound as a book that sits alongside Dr. Seuss in the school library. On 4.7-inch screens, kids play games like Madden, where they get to be owner and coach of their own team. A middle school boy starts a website where he posts the most popular songs and albums each week and then asks people to vote. In the first year, four thousand people cast a vote. There is a seventeen-year-old YouTuber who attracts millions of followers and earns a hefty paycheck from advertisers. A young girl starts making all-natural cosmetics and not only establishes a company but also ignites a movement. *When these same kids go to church, they are keenly aware of the contrast when their role simply amounts to being a receiver and participator.*

Researcher Richard Learner defines *thriving* as the goal for healthy adolescent development. Thriving is the result of a positive developmental trajectory where teens become adult contributors to civil society.[7] According to William Damon, developing purpose is a key component of thriving. *Purpose* means discovering ways to contribute that are larger than yourself and participating in activities toward this end.[8] When young people discern their purpose and can contribute meaningfully to this purpose, they are on the road to thriving. Isn't thriving of this kind also our vision for young people in the church? Imagine young people in your church discovering God's purposes and exploring ways they can meaningfully contribute with their lives both in the church and more broadly in society.

In collectivist societies, purpose is received from the community (which can be for good or ill). Yet purpose must be discovered in individualistic societies. I would also argue that when consuming is a condition, young people will tire of consumption, which in turn will lead to a hunger for purpose. In support of my theory, researchers suggest that younger generations are increasingly drawn toward social activism.[9] Might this demonstrate a longing to contribute to something larger than self? Maybe this is a sign that consuming does not quench their thirst. Young people are created *for* God and God's purposes. The church's call is to empower them toward this end and enable them to discover ways they might contribute to God's redemptive work in the world.

When communities value contribution, a young person's potential for God will thrive.

PRACTICE SEEING POTENTIAL

Adjust what you see and look for potential. Adjusting what we see in young people beyond their specific actions and attitudes will take intentional effort because it is a paradigm change. Young people are God's valuable creation with potential *for* God as contributors to God's redemptive movement. Maybe we need to recognize and evaluate our fears and even confess how these fears are blurring our vision of young people. This will impact the content we teach, the type of programs we offer, and even how we engage with them. When we look for potential, our fears for young people will morph into hope, and our fixing posture will evolve into empowerment. Recognizing potential changes our expectations and relationships. Researchers at Search Institute argue that nothing has a stronger impact on young people than positive relationships where young people experience the following five relationship elements. Each one of these focuses on em-

> **Our fears for young people will morph into hope, and our fixing posture will evolve into empowerment.**

powerment and potential while also providing the nurture and care young people need.[10]

- *Express care*—showing I matter by being dependable, listening, believing in me, showing warmth, and giving encouragement

- *Challenge growth*—pushing me to grow by expecting the best, stretching me, providing accountability, and helping me reflect on failures

- *Provide support*—working with me to complete tasks and achieve goals, navigating life's difficulties together, empowering and advocating for me, and setting boundaries

- *Share power*—respecting me, letting me speak, working to include my ideas, collaborating, and giving me opportunities to lead

- *Expand possibilities*—connecting me with people and places outside my experiences, broadening my horizons, and inspiring me with future possibilities

Teach about God's redemptive movement. Pull together a list of what your youth ministry taught last year. How frequently are you teaching the big picture? For young people to imagine themselves as contributors, they need to regularly swim in the story of God's redemptive movement in the world. This gospel story does not end with their salvation from sin. Rather, this is the basis for explaining that they are freed *for* God. In your community, how are you presently expressing that we are free for God? What language, phrases, practices, and teachings can you build on and include in your regular teaching lineup? This can become a story line that heightens a young person's imagination and offers a vision for the world beyond what they presently see. This framework also allows young people to practice discerning God's activity in the world.[11]

Point out specific sparks. Point out unique gifts or character traits that you see in each young person. Peter Scales calls this looking for a person's *spark*, which is defined as "a fire in an adolescent's life, providing energy, joy, purpose, and direction."[12] Researchers conclude that adults can ignite a spark by helping youth identify, name, and discover ways to use their gifts to contribute to society. For young people in the church, this entails helping them make connections between the spark and God's redemptive movement in the world. This is easier to do with explicit talents. Libby is an artist and can teach classes in the church's ministry to at-risk kids. Morris is a musician who can join the worship team and introduce them to his musical style. But many sparks are not as apparent.

James is an active seventh grader who moves faster and talks louder than his peers. Every week at church someone has to ask him to slow down, lower his voice, and watch for others. Today Ms. Collins, a long-time member of the church, hears him coming. She is already irritated because she knows she will have to remind him to settle down yet again. All of a sudden, James hits the brakes. Standing before him is a little boy crying because he has dropped his snack all over the floor. As if by impulse, James gently puts his hand on the boy's shoulder and quietly reassures him. Together they pick up the scattered food, and James is off again at full speed. Ms. Collins meets him at the door. Her demeanor shifts, and now she is the one putting her hand on James's shoulder. Telling him what she witnessed, she says, "James, you just showed tremendous compassion and gentleness to that boy. Imagine how God might use this gift in the world." Take in the power of these simple sentences for a kid like James, who is likely used to hearing that he is a problem. Helping young people discover their spark is not about starting a program or giving them a strengths quiz, even if these are helpful. Sparks are seen in real life. But we will only see them when we are looking for potential.

Be space makers. Valuing contribution means creating opportunities for kids to exercise, practice, and grow their sparks alongside adults. If we believe young people have a growing capacity to contribute to the church, this should show up in a youth-ministry mission statement as well as frame the programs and activities. In addition to helping them grow in their faith, how can you enable them to contribute to your *church's mission* in new ways?

I am sitting with the missions committee seeking approval to take a group of kids to Mexico. We plan to work with a partner church in the Yucatan that is building a new school. A committee member asks, "Why do you need to take them so far away when there is so much work to do right here?" I am prepared for this question and have ready what I think is a great answer. I declare, "Young people need to be removed from their daily lives in order to experience God and learn to serve others." An elderly gentleman at the end of the table groans and points out that I just made these kids the central purpose of the trip. He challenges me by replying, "Have you read the church's mission statement? We are committed to serving the global church. These kids are more than able to contribute to the church's mission. If you want them to experience God, stay here. But if you want them to join God's work in the world, take them to Mexico." This man sees young people as capable contributors to the church's mission while I limit my focus to their faith (and a really irresponsible view of missions).

Based on a large research sample of middle and high school youth, Peter Scales concludes that there is a significant gap between those who are able to identify their spark and those who receive help to develop it.[13] Some 66 to 80 percent of youth can name a personal spark while less than half "experience relational opportunities to develop" this spark. These statistics become more alarming when compared to other research that indicates only 10 percent of adults have a "strongly favorable personal attitude toward engaging adolescents outside of their families."[14] Adults who make space for young people in churches and ministries can fill in this gap.

It is much easier to adjust our lens and look for a young person's potential. Identifying sparks will likely be pretty rewarding. But making space? This asks us to share power and take risks. Sometimes making space for young people is difficult because our investment in the church is deeply meaningful, and we do not want to give it up. Other times we resist making space for young people because we grimace at their ideas.

A 2014 General Electric commercial captures this well. The scene opens with the birth of an unrecognizable, furry creature who serves as a metaphor for new ideas. We see glimpses of "New Ideas" growing up, not fitting in, experiencing ridicule, and finally being ousted from the typical business world. All the while, the narrator tells a story. "Ideas are scary. They come into this world ugly and messy. Ideas are frightening because they threaten what is known. They are the natural-born enemy of the way things are. Yes, ideas are scary and messy and fragile. But under the proper care, they become something beautiful."

I am not sure the furry creature actually becomes beautiful, but the commercial's point is effective. The contributions young people imagine often do feel ugly and scary. They can also feel threatening to our way of doing things or how we have understood what God's movement among us should look like. I am not advocating that we release all control and trade places with young people so they can try out every new idea they have. I am reminding us that God is bigger than our adult conceptions. Guarding the church's way of doing things with white knuckles will diminish the Spirit's movement. Remember that a primary avenue for God's transformation among us is through relationships. We need to listen, value, nuance, take risks, and make space for young people to contribute their "new ideas." They need us, and we need them. Being space makers empowers young people to exercise and practice their potential. Ways to contribute need to be tried on and worked out. If we are honest, this is actually what all of us are doing. Some of us just have more practice. In the end, when young people see how their sparks contribute to the church's wider mission, they will experience belonging. Maybe then they will also stop leaving the church behind.

Let's change the epidemic narrative. Young people are not problems to solve. God created them with potential to contribute to God's redemptive purposes among us. Christ frees them from sin so that they are free *for* God. When we value contribution, a young person's potential for God will thrive and flourish.

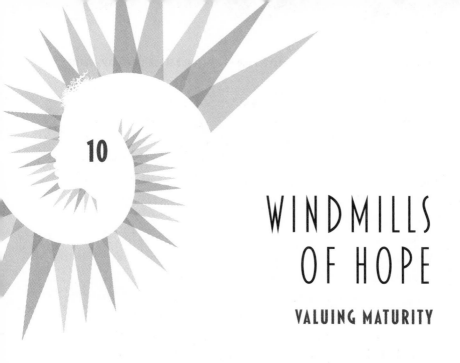

WINDMILLS
OF HOPE

VALUING MATURITY

WHY IS IT THAT MY FRIENDS AT SCHOOL and the adults where I work act better than the people in this church?" Jessie gets straight to the point as we cross paths in the parking lot. His church is in the middle of a nasty court case fighting over which side of the church will "win" the property. My mind quickly processes potential answers. Should I make this about sin? "Being a Christian doesn't mean we do everything right." What about giving a wider perspective? "Christians have always disagreed about what faith looks like in life." Maybe I should just turn it back to Jessie? "Take the plank out of your own eye before you cast judgment on others." Since none of these answers are remotely adequate, I keep my mouth shut and shake my head in sad agreement.

What is at the core of Jessie's anger? It is really not about the church split or even the property. He is angry because those who claim to be Christians are not exhibiting Christ's love in their actions. Jessie expects more from them, and he is right to be disappointed. It is nothing new for Christians to be characterized as hypocrites. There has been and always will be a discrepancy between the faith we express and our actions until we experience God's grace in the ultimate community. However, younger generations have a distinct response to this gap.

We have a new word in our vocabulary: the *nones*. In 2012, Pew Research began to use this term to characterize the growing segment of the US population who, when asked about their religious affiliation, checks the box "unaffiliated." *None* is now a common shorthand descriptor. In part, this trend corresponds to a decrease in the number of Americans who are "religiously active" (e.g., attend religious services, pray). It is also true that millennials are more likely than other generations to make this claim.[1] Among older millennials (born 1981–1989), 25 percent identified as unaffiliated in 2007 and 34 percent by 2014. The younger millennials (born 1990–1996) were first surveyed by Pew in 2014, and 36 percent claimed to be "unaffiliated" with a religious organization. Pew researcher Gregory Smith predicts this trend will continue: "Millennials, who make up a growing share of the population as they reach adulthood and older Americans die off, are far less religiously observant than the older cohorts."[2] Smith was correct; these numbers still appear to be growing today, and this trend is coupled with an increased number of young people who identify as atheists.[3]

One of the top reasons those surveyed give for checking the unaffiliated box is "dislike of religious institutions." Researchers work to explain this phenomenon and often conclude that younger generations are suspicious of authority. For example, in his 2011 book *You Lost Me: Why Young Christians Are Leaving the Church and Rethinking the Faith*, Barna's David Kinnaman cites increased skepticism of authority as one reason young people are leaving the church.[4] He explains this as a cultural shift and the consequence of secular society's devaluing of religion in general. This confirms psychologist Jeffrey

Arnett's earlier finding, yet Arnett clarifies that emerging adults today are not angry with institutions as much as they place a higher value on their own individual experiences.[5] He states, "They tended to view participation in any institution as a compromise of their individuality."[6] Being suspicious of authority is a secondary outcome of their prioritization of *my* experience. Rather than equating young people who walk away from churches to a 1960s anti-authority protest, the basis for walking away is likely more closely aligned with the experience they have with the institution.

Add to this what we explored earlier about complex societies. Religious institutions must now have a specialization. Unlike other eras, churches no longer have authority across multiple sectors of society, and by default "spirituality" has become our specialty. Whether or not a church's spiritual product is personally satisfying or meets a person's felt needs is often the basis for evaluating a church or youth ministry. If we are not careful, churches can end up working hard to attract people based on personal preferences in order to keep the lights on rather than attending to who we are becoming as God's people. Jessie's anger expresses the culmination of these factors. He is looking for the real thing—evidence of Christ's transforming work in a Christian community. When his experience does not match this, disillusionment sets in.

> **If we are not careful, churches can end up working hard to attract people based on personal preferences in order to keep the lights on rather than attending to who we are becoming as God's people.**

What does all of this mean? It would be a shame if we were to conclude that every young person we meet distrusts authority and dislikes the church. Instead, let's recognize and build on the deep value young people place on their experiences with Christian communities. Subsequently, rising generations are more apt than prior generations to decide for themselves if beliefs, people, and communities are worthy of trust and commitment. Here is the silver lining: the reverse is also likely to be true. When communities reflect the Spirit's transforming presence and power, rising generations may be more apt to trust and commit to communities of faith.

I am aware that my emphasis on Christian community in this book makes differences and dissensions among us more glaring. Focusing on what we *should be* feels like a fantasy that we will never experience. On top of this, being a community is the hard choice. Living apart from community or with the like-minded is much easier. Social media platforms provide this opportunity by recycling our preferred ideologies among groups and people we choose to follow. However, to live in community is to commit to being together where, in the words of Dietrich Bonhoeffer, we encounter differing wills. This is not just about who likes stir-fry versus sushi or who unwinds by binge-watching Netflix versus eating ice cream. Christian community is not the fellowship of sameness but always difference, which will result in conflict. And I have said nothing so far about sin. Add this to the mix, and we know we are a huge mess. I hope that hearing the word *community* makes you squirm, as it does me. For, certainly, as soon as we declare ourselves a Christian community, we see how we fail.

At the same time, our hope resides in the signs of Christ's ongoing transforming work among us. Maybe we miss seeing Christ's activity because we pay more attention to the conflicts. Or might it also be that growth as a community is not on our radar? Think about this in light of what we explored earlier. When consuming is a condition, religion offers personal spirituality, and community is voluntary, Christianity is prone to tilt toward personal experiences rather than pressing us toward the difficult, time-consuming, and long road toward maturity. We must resist this tendency.

Christianity cannot be reduced to a story about *me* and God's plans for my life without also recognizing our shared identity as a people belonging to God. Christian communities should be places where we anticipate Christ's transforming activity through the Spirit and make this central to the church's mission and purpose. If Christians have a shared identity, and Christian communities have a vital purpose, then maturing as persons and as a community will be a core value. We will gather for a vital purpose: to practice living like the reconciled people we will one day be. Our differing wills become a primary avenue for Christ's ongoing work among us as the Spirit's presence and power frees us personally and as a community *for* God. When this happens, churches act as signs drawing people's attention to God and proclaiming God's redemptive movement among us. Let's resist the defeatist attitude that says there will always be a gap between what we profess and how we live. The result will be giving in to our untransformed lives, and younger generations are sure to notice. Instead, let's learn what valuing maturity looks like and put it into practice in our churches.

As I unpack the value *maturity*, you will notice that I focus on the whole community rather than just youth ministry and young people. The first step to caring for rising generations involves local churches and minis-

Christianity cannot be reduced to a story about *me* and God's plans for my life without also recognizing our shared identity as a people belonging to God.

tries prioritizing their shared identity and purpose as God's people. Only when we make this shift will young people experience firsthand Christ's movement in our midst.

MATURITY AS BURGEONING GROWTH

In Pauline letters we come across a word often translated as "mature." Other translations use the words *complete* or *perfect*.[7] To be mature casts an eschatological vision of God redeeming all things. This is our hope: all will be complete and perfect. At first glance, to be mature is pretty daunting. Yet as New Testament authors speak of being mature, they also include a call for the readers to put into practice now what they *anticipate* will ultimately be perfect or complete. For example, in Philippians 3:12-16 the author challenges the reader to "press on" now and move toward the "prize" that will be awarded in the future by putting into practice what they have already learned (v. 12). The "mature" (v. 15) are those who start practicing now. To be mature in this way is to be maturing toward complete maturity.

Even so, it is difficult to conceive of maturing as only progressive. A single line gradually angling upward like an arrow showing population growth does not quite capture our experiences. Mike Yaconnelli wrote a book titled *Messy Spirituality*, in which he takes our conception of spiritual growth as a straight, upward-angled progressive line and makes it look more like a roller-coaster.[8] We resonate with this personally, and the same is true for a community.

The word *burgeoning* better captures what the New Testament authors convey. Burgeoning growth implies the process of growth that is expansive, multivaried, and flourishing with anticipation. Imagine a tree's growth over time. Its roots stretch down while its branches reach up. Some upward growth is cut off to increase new growth. Disease cuts off some of the roots. The tree bears fruit or flowers. Seasons change, leaves fall off, and then spring's tender green leaves appear. Burgeoning maturity is varied and expansive, not linear or consistently progressive.

Growing in love. Maturing in the Pauline letters also implies growth similar to our biological development, like a child maturing into an adult. Paul reflects, "When I was a child, I talked like a child, I thought like a child, I reasoned like a child. When I became a man, I put the ways of childhood behind me" (1 Corinthians 13:11). Yet Christian maturity is not just any kind of growth. A closer look at 1 Corinthians 13 reveals that the author is defining the eternal nature of God's love, which does not fail.[9] Paul promises, "Love never fails. But where there are prophecies, they will cease; where there are tongues, they will be stilled; where there is knowledge, it will pass away" (v. 8). Since God's love endures, love will also mark the Corinthians' "completeness" (v. 10). In light of this, the author admonishes the Corinthians to "stop thinking like children . . . but in your thinking be adults" (1 Corinthians 14:20). They should be maturing in their love for one another.

It would be nice if this came about by waving some kind of spiritual magic wand. Nothing could be further from the truth. Instead, the Corinthians receive a practical to-do (and not-to-do) list. Paul tells them, "Love is patient, love is kind. It does not envy, it does not boast, it is not proud. It does not dishonor others, it is not self-seeking, it is not easily angered, it keeps no record of wrongs. Love does not delight in evil but rejoices with the truth. It always protects, always trusts, always hopes, always perseveres" (1 Corinthians 13:4-7). Growth that characterizes *maturing* is learning how to act in loving ways. Love as a solo venture, even love of self, does not make this list. Love is expressed in relationship. As the Corinthians' love for one another grows, they are maturing toward the ultimate community where love for God and one another will be complete. This again attests to the fact that relationships are a primary avenue for transformation in the Christian community.

A challenge to act maturely. Pastors and New Testament scholars alike remind us to pay attention to Paul's use of *therefore* in the text. It is as if Paul is waving a giant flag to grab our attention. A *therefore* marks a letter's shift from proclamation about Christ to a declaration of the community's responsibility. This means the gospel has ethical implications. When we read that the church is a body (Colossians 3:15), one in Spirit (Ephesians 4:4) or a people (1 Corinthians 1:2), the *therefore*s are challenges to act accordingly. *Therefore*, "love must be sincere. Hate what is evil; cling to what is good. Be devoted to one another in love. Honor one another above yourselves" (Romans 12:9-10). *Therefore*, since you have been raised with Christ, take off these vices and put on these virtues (Colossians 3:1-17). Since we Christians have a shared identity—*therefore* we are called to act like a people, to function like a body where each part is valued, and to become a temple of the Holy Spirit where the Spirit dwells. We are called to be a sign, which points past us to God and God's redemptive movement in our midst (John 17). Yet to be considered a sign, we must be an authentic sign. This will take our cooperation.

Remembering that we have a shared identity means adding to our personal discipleship a commitment to community discipleship. Alongside seeking to be personally transformed, we must also commit to the community's transformation. I do not mean this is an either-or—a focus on *either* personal discipleship *or* community discipleship. This is a both/and. God's purposes include *both* persons *and* communities who increasingly reflect love of God and neighbor. Just as we have a shared identity, we all share this responsibility. It is equally yours and mine, young and old. We already explored the vital purpose for our relationships with one another—reconciled relationship. A reciprocal church values maturity by taking seriously our responsibility to practice reconciliation.

Remembering that we have a shared identity means adding to our personal discipleship a commitment to community discipleship

Let's turn our attention to three community-forming practices drawn from the fruit of the Spirit in Galatians 5.

PRACTICE RECONCILIATION

The author of Galatians seeks to resolve a conflict in some of the early churches. Clearly, the inability to live peaceably as Christ's community is a perpetual problem. There are some among them strongly advocating that the Gentiles continue following the Jewish law by being circumcised. We can interpret their intent as good because they understood the law as a means for eradicating sin.[10] They were trusting in the law as part of the covenant promise. But the author boldly pronounces this view to be a perversion of the gospel of Christ (Galatians 1:7). Instead, we experience liberty in Christ and should focus on the original intent of the law—to love others.[11] As a result, Christ's liberating power has social implications. Paul names specific relationships that need liberation in these churches: the ethnic separation between Jews and Greeks; the economic and social separation between slave and free; and the gender divisions among males and females (Galatians 3:28).

Against this relational backdrop, the author employs a cosmic vision defining a battle between the flesh (or sinful nature) and the Spirit (Galatians 5:17).[12] The cross is a liberating event that resolves this battle by breaking the powerful forces holding humanity captive.[13] This is not a cross that frees us to be autonomous from one another. This cross liberates us *for* one another s*o that disruptive relationships have the opportunity to practice reconciliation.* After all, this is God's purpose for our relationships with one another in the community of faith.

The Spirit, windmills, and generating fruit. Two lists in the text contrast what the flesh and the Spirit produce.[14] The acts of the flesh are those characteristics that destroy community (Galatians 5:19-20): sexual immorality, hatred, discord, jealousy, fits of rage, selfish ambition, and factions among groups. Conversely, the Spirit generates life-giving or nutrient-rich fruit for the community.[15] Paul says, "But the fruit of the Spirit is love, joy, peace, forbearance, kindness, goodness, faithfulness, gentleness and self-control. Against such things there is no law. Those who belong to Christ Jesus have crucified the flesh with its passions and desires. Since we live by the Spirit, let us keep in step with the Spirit" (5:22-25). Make note that in this passage we do not produce the fruit. The Spirit produces fruit. This is important. However, the Spirit does not coerce or force us to act in fruit-bearing ways. We retain our agency and wills. We have to accept the invitation to "keep in step with the Spirit." Alone, our efforts will not be enough. Our hope is that we join the movement of the Spirit, who produces community-nurturing fruit.

I imagine the Spirit's work to be like the wind captured by a wind turbine. Whether they converge with a city skyline or dominate wide-open spaces, I am always struck by how slowly windmills turn, as if only a little wind generates significant power. (Mechanically minded readers, hang with me for a moment and remember I am a theologian not an engineer.) What I do not know, omniscient Google does. I learned two important things about windmills. First, the blade's design increases the potential for receiving the wind. The blades are always attached at an angle. If the wind were to hit the blade bluntly, the blade would act like a shield and the wind would bounce off and move past the blade. Instead, the angle allows the blade to catch the wind as it rushes by and causes the blade's motion. In addition, the blade's surface is uneven in order to disrupt the wind's path and guide it toward the angled blade. *The blades are designed to receive the wind.* Second, windmills have an internal mechanism of turning gears. These gears transform the rotation created by the wind to create a faster rotation for generating energy.

Relationships have the potential to be like windmills by harnessing the Spirit's power. The otherness, differences, and conflicts among us are similar to the angled and uneven surfaces of the blades. What feels negative and disruptive actually reveals possibility, because *relationships are a primary avenue for our transformation.* Once we angle our lives to receive the wind, the Spirit can generate the fruit needed to nourish the community: love, joy, peace, forbearance, kindness, goodness, faithfulness, gentleness, and self-control. But the Spirit does not coerce. We must lean into the power of the Spirit—angling ourselves and our rough surfaces toward the Spirit. There is no guarantee here. We will still act in deeply hurtful and even hateful ways. We will not fully overcome our community-disruptive behaviors until God's grace permeates the ultimate community. Even so, the cross's liberating power holds implications that include taking responsibility for the negative impact we have on one another and working to live at peace. We are not left to carry this out alone.

The Spirit's superhuman movement among us makes the impossible possible. Like the windmill's turning gears, the Spirit generates far more power than we can generate ourselves. The wind of the Spirit aligns with God's purposes and produces fruit we desperately need to nourish community. As difficult and even impossible as this appears, we must ask: how might we tilt our rough surfaces toward the Spirit?

Let's look at three specific practices that act as first steps toward the ultimate reconciliation we long and hope for.

Curiosity generates patience. To bear with one another, the Spirit produces forbearance or patience. How can we join with the Spirit's work? We can practice curiosity when relationships are disruptive.

There is a loud knock at my office door. The father's fiery eyes and clenched jaw need little interpretation—I am about to get blasted. He accuses, "How dare you interfere in my relationship with my son." Genuine bewilderment accompanies the sick feeling in my stomach. Backstory: At youth group last night, his son, Andy, offers to meet up with a couple girls later to smoke weed. As you might imagine, the chatter moves through the group and quickly reaches me. I confront him. Smoking pot is a new thing for Andy, and he is pretty scared about getting in trouble. I present two options: "Either you tell your parents about this, or I will go with you to tell your parents." He chooses the solo path. I expect Andy's dad to thank me for caring for his son. Instead, furious eyes are accusing me of violating his parental duty. From his perspective I put him in a situation where his response to Andy might backfire and have a lifelong negative impact on their relationship. He threatens, "I'm taking this to the elders and demanding they get rid of you. You are a danger to every kid in this church." He slams the door behind him.

My heart beats wildly, and the "flight or fight" instinct drives my response. Self-preservation is my goal. I call two elders, explain my side of the story, and gain their assurance that my job is not on the line. Next, I call three adult volunteers who had been on the scene. I explain the dad's reaction and threats and do not hang up until I have their support. My phone calls continue: my husband, my mom, my sister, my friend—everyone empathizes with me, and I imagine them all putting on battle gear ready to defend me. Over the next year, every time I see this dad in the church's hallways, my heart starts racing, and I avoid him as if my life depends on it.

I resist being curious. The disruption stays at the forefront, and self-protection prevails. As you read about this incident, it begs for more information, doesn't it? His anger and fears are irrational and make no sense. Clearly, there is more driving his outburst than me calling his son out for pot smoking. But I do not know what this is because I am resisting curiosity. I can only see the attack and do not pause to look for what is lurking just beneath his anger. What remains is a disrupted relationship. In retrospect, had I practiced curiosity, the space between us might have opened up for more conversation. This dad was upset and needed me to be patient with him, which I obviously did not offer. Could the Spirit have produced fruit to nurture this relationship?

Being patient with one another is rather essential for a community, isn't it? We act in ways that disappoint. We react to each other without thinking. We project feelings and experiences onto one another, often without even realizing it. Practicing curiosity means looking for what is behind a person's words or actions. It means being confident that there are reasons unknown to me that drive the person and maybe recognizing that this is not just about me. Being curious is more than just giving the person the benefit of the doubt. We can draw from positive psychology on this point.[16] Curiosity starts with two simultaneous affirmations:

1. You (who overreacts, disappoints, and projects your stuff onto me) are generally doing the best that you can do with the abilities, knowledge, and resources you have at the time.

2. You (who overreacts, disappoints, and projects your stuff onto me) can do better.

These affirmations recognize our common brokenness and dependence on our Creator. There is no intent here to ignore wrongdoing or cover up a person's behavior. *You can do better.* Instead, to affirm both of these statements asks us to look at the whole person rather than reducing someone to their poor behavior. Being curious allows us to wonder what would compel this person to act so rudely or aggressively. Practicing curiosity opens up the space between us for more conversation. When we do, *the Spirit* can generate patience. Patience is needed because sometimes we only see part of what is going on in a situation, while others might have a wider view. Patience is needed because those that you look up to will disappoint you. Patience is needed because those you wish to lead will not always follow. My sin and your sin have consequences on our relationship. I will hurt you. You will disappoint me. Is it also generally true that we both are doing our best with our present abilities, knowledge and resources? At the same time, each of us can do better. When we practice curiosity, we angle our rough-edged relationship blades toward the wind of the Spirit, who generates what is impossible to produce by ourselves—patience. Learning patience is also taking one step toward reconciliation.

Fasting generates self-control. In Galatians 5, Paul emphasizes Christ's liberating freedom from the law. He also cautions, "You, my brothers and sisters, were called to be free. But do not use your freedom to indulge the flesh; rather, serve one another humbly in love" (Galatians 5:13). Our liberty in Christ is intended for building up the body, not for self-gratification. Excessive self-indulgence characterizes what the flesh produces: jealousy, fits of rage, selfish ambition, and drunkenness. Contrast this with the Spirit generating self-control. Paul writes, "For the entire law is fulfilled in keeping this one command: 'Love your neighbor as yourself.' If you bite and devour each other, watch out or you will be destroyed by each other" (Galatians 5:14-15). Self-indulgence destroys community. Self-control nurtures the community and acts as another step toward reconciliation. How might we join with the Spirit's work?

Fasting is a historic practice in the church that takes many forms in our day, from limiting food intake to fasting from technology. Both require giving up or going without to be set free *for* God. For example, when we limit our food intake and feel hungry, we are free to experience our dependence on God. Fasting also addresses our tendency toward overindulgence. Limiting screen access recognizes our culture's distractedness and sets us free to give God our full attention.

Freedom is the benefit of fasting according to St. John Chrysostom, fourth-century archbishop of Constantinople. In a homily addressing Christians who fear fasting, he warns them that the real fear is drunkenness and gluttony (both rooted in self-gratification and overindulgence). These bind "our hands behind our backs and surrenders us as slaves and captives to the tyranny of the passions . . . Fasting, however, who finds us slaves and prisoners, loosens the bonds and delivers us from the tyranny; she restores us to our former freedom."[17] As Galatians 5 warns, Christ does not free us for self-gratification, which ironically leads to captivity. Christ liberates us to serve others. Defining freedom that includes limiting self is difficult for us to grasp. In America in particular, our emphasis on personal freedom can overshadow Paul's description of the freedom we have in Christ.

I live in the great state of New Hampshire, whose motto is "Live free or die." Believe me, this motto is alive and well. As you cross Massachusetts's border into the state on a sunny day, you see lines of motorcyclists removing their helmets. New Hampshire does not have a law requiring helmets. As they ride off with hair blowing in the wind, I hear an interpretation of the motto. It is as if they are saying, "I'm going to live free or die while doing so." The phrase originated during the Revolutionary War and was intended to be a firm declaration

In Christ, we too gain a collective freedom rather than unabated individual rights.

against England's heavy-handed political control. The phrase did not emphasize individual freedom—"get off my lawn"—but the colonists' call for their collective freedom from an oppressive nation. In Christ, we too gain a collective freedom rather than unabated individual rights. Such freedom sometimes requires limiting self-interest and forgoing self-gratification.

In no way am I claiming Christians should act meekly in the face of oppression or wrongdoing. This is not a call for a false

Christian humility where Christians do not declare or proclaim their beliefs strongly. Limiting our freedom does not mean asking a woman to stay with an abusive husband or quieting voices that address racial or gender injustices. I am questioning freedom that celebrates self-interest, not rightly seeking protection and justice for self or others.

In Galatians 5, I imagine Paul calling us to fast from our personal freedom—for a time—to weigh whether our actions nurture the community. Are we acting in self-interest? Am I being overindulgent? Am I using my freedom in Christ to build the body? Fasting itself can become self-indulgent. Fasts are meant to be broken. If you go without food for too long, you will die. The intent is to break the pattern and limit our freedom by going without for a time in order to be free. Fasting helps us pause, seek God, and discern how even our good intentions might have negative implications for others. What action will best serve the body?

- silence or speaking
- posting on social media or meeting for coffee
- sacrificing or asserting
- confronting or turning the other cheek

Fasting allows us to pause, step back, weigh outcomes, choose words, and open up space for the Spirit to nurture community. When we practice fasting, we angle our rough-edged relationship blades toward the wind of the Spirit, who generates what is difficult to produce ourselves—self-control. Self-control is an essential step toward reconciliation.

Forgiving generates love. I am sitting in class listening to a presentation on forgiveness by three African American students.[18] They are evaluating a view of forgiveness promoted by cultural icon Oprah Winfrey. She defines forgiveness as "letting go" to "allow self to move to full presence," so we can "embrace now, not hold on to what is the past." This form of forgiveness promises to benefit individual health and bring personal fulfillment. My students boldly challenge this perspective as overindividualized and ineffective. In their words, me feeling good "makes no difference in a world full of racism, police brutality, and mass shootings."

Instead, they walk us through biblical texts that link the practice of forgiveness to God's larger purpose of reconciliation. My eyes fix on the screen as they project the words of Martin Luther King Jr.: "Love is the only force capable of transforming an enemy into a friend. We never get rid of an enemy by meeting hate with hate: we get rid of an enemy by getting rid of enmity. By its very nature, hate destroys and tears down; by its very nature, love creates and builds up. Love transforms with redemptive power."[19] One of the students concludes, "Your transgressor's future depends on you forgiving them." These students understand God's purpose for Christian community includes learning to forgive as a beginning step toward practicing reconciliation. In the Sermon on the Mount, Matthew writes of Jesus' teaching about the law "do not murder." The law establishes fitting behavior for people belonging to God, and Jesus raises the bar, telling them to focus on the implications of the law and not just the law itself. Jesus asserts, "Therefore, if you are offering your gift at the altar and there remember that your brother or sister has something against you, leave your gift there in front of the altar. First go and be reconciled to them; then come and offer your gift" (Matthew 5:23-24).

Dietrich Bonhoeffer gives us practical advice on how to practice forgiveness.[20] When a brother or sister in Christ sins against me, before I look at this person, I should imagine Christ standing between us. Seeing Christ immediately produces thankfulness in me because of what Christ has done for me. Only then can I look at the person who is the cause of my pain because Christ stands between us. The same forgiveness Christ extends to me is the forgiveness I can extend to my brother or sister. Bonhoeffer describes thankfulness for Christ's forgiveness as the only starting point to forgiving each other.

There is nothing here that waters down sin's consequences or re-
duces the pain and suffering caused by even those closest to us. There
is nothing here that says we should ignore or gloss over the hurt we
feel or cause. The opposite is true—this takes the real effects of sin
seriously. We are not a perfect community. We are a forgiven community made righteous (in right relationship) only through Christ's
self-giving love. This love is ever active in Christ as the Spirit does for
us what we cannot do for ourselves. I will add one piece to my student's wise words: "Your transgressor's future depends on you forgiving them. A Christian community's future depends on the practice
of forgiveness." When we practice forgiveness, we angle our rough-
edged relationship blades toward the wind of the Spirit who produces
love among us.

Building windmills. There is no single answer as to why people,
especially among rising generations, increasingly check the box "unaffiliated" next to religious affiliation. What we do know is that, unlike
past generations, individuality and personal experiences among young
people supersede their loyalty to institutions, and this includes our
churches. Now more than ever before, we need to add community-
forming practices to our discipleship efforts. We are called to be maturing communities of faith. Valuing maturity anticipates that one day
God's grace will enable us to be fully mature. Burgeoning maturing is
expansive, multivaried, and flourishing with anticipation. We are maturing when we turn our lives in this direction. Growth involves
learning to act in loving ways. This is our call and responsibility as a
community with a shared identity. We are a people belonging to God
and existing for God's purposes. When our relationships transform,
we act as an authentic sign of God's reconciling love.

Churches are made up of real people in real relationships. It is a
guarantee that there will be disruptions where our differing wills and
sin's consequences can literally destroy us. Yet our rough-edged relationships are designed for receiving the Spirit's generating power to
help us do what we cannot do for ourselves. The Spirit produces

community-nurturing fruit. But we will not be forced. Let's work together to receive the Spirit's power by practicing curiosity and growing in our capacity to be patient with one another. We can practice fasting from our personal freedom in order to discern whether self-interest motivates our words or actions, and the Spirit will generate self-control. Forgiveness is a crucial step toward reconciliation, which is God's purpose for Christian community. Even in our weak and feeble efforts to forgive, the Spirit can powerfully generate maturing love among us.

Building a windmill farm is a massive undertaking requiring trained engineers, million-dollar budgets, and skilled workers. When it is complete, the skyline fills with angled, rough-edged blades designed to receive the wind so the generators can kick in and produce energy. Imagine Spirit-generated relationships in our churches filling the skyline of our cities and towns, and proclaiming the transforming, redeeming love of God among us. In the words of hymn writer Peter Scholtes, then "they will know we are Christians by our love."

FAITH FLOURISHES
WITH PRACTICE

YOU LIKELY PICKED UP THIS BOOK because you know too many young people who didn't flourish in your youth ministry or church. There appears to be a widening gap between all our efforts to build strong youth ministries and an increased number among rising generations who claim labels like the *dones*, the *nones*, and the *spiritual but not religious*.

We've examined the culture landscape. We are swimming in an overindividualized culture where we choose the communities we belong to and conceive of religion as just another product in the marketplace for our spiritual consumption. These waters influence our expectations of the church and perceptions of each other. Emphasizing *me* and *my choices* influences our practices, dispositions, and expectations, reducing the church's role to another consumable product and *people* to tools for personal discipleship. With good intent, we double our efforts to create more and better programs to support young people's faith. Youth ministries, and more specifically all adults who work tirelessly with young people, rise and fall under this pressure. Good sociological research will continue to discover key factors contributing to those with long-lasting faith commitments, but this research alone won't remind us of our shared identity as a people belonging to God. Come to find out, eating melon on Tuesdays didn't save us.

Have these pages awakened you to the good news? Rising generations are already tired of consuming and long to discover a purpose outside themselves. As they walk away from churches, their footsteps plead for those of us who remain inside to demonstrate the love we proclaim. Younger generations await more than adults trying to grab their attention with the latest and greatest. They long to be in communities where they experience God's presence in reconciling relationships. What we call a crisis may well be a prophetic moment. But don't move too quickly. Moving forward first requires our confession for the unintended consequences of our—God's people's—actions in the lives of so many people. A time of lament is an appropriate first step.[1]

We can reclaim a full gospel message. God's presence with us confirms our shared identity and vital purpose as a people belonging to God. Christ is redeeming persons and communities. Christ's self-giving love reconciles us to God *and* others. Our relationships are an avenue for the Spirit's activity. We experience the inconceivable: our differences are opportunities for the Spirit.

In Paul's letters, Christian communities possess a unique trait. God's movement among them includes generating and maintaining unity. The implausible Jew and Gentile unity declared in Ephesians 2:11-20 casts a future vision that reaches into our lives now. God is creating a new humanity, a spiritual temple, and a people by removing barriers and "dividing walls of hostility" (v. 14) through Christ by the Spirit. The result is "peace" (v. 17). This isn't illusory or other-worldly spiritual unity. This is God's purpose for relationships among Christians in local gatherings in real life.

Relationships are a primary avenue for this transformation, and the Spirit's power is our source to practice living as a reconciled people until we are part of the ultimate community. The Spirit's presence dwells with us powerfully, making the impossible possible: a maturing body.

> Then we will no longer be infants, tossed back and forth by the waves, and blown here and there by every wind of teaching and by the cunning and craftiness of people in their deceitful scheming. Instead, speaking the truth in love, we will grow to become in every respect the *mature* body of him who is the head, that is, Christ. From him the whole body, joined and held together by every supporting ligament, grows and builds itself up in love, as each part does its work. (Ephesians 4:14-16; italics added)

In the moments when this happens, our churches proclaim God's glory, and others might find hope in God's redeeming love. Without this broader vision, emphasizing community in our churches and ministries will become self-enclosed and self-focused. Instead, we hope to proclaim God's redeeming love and join God's vital purposes to reach beyond our communities into all corners of the world.

Alongside the declining number of Christians in the United States and especially those among rising generations, there are other sets of numbers requiring our attention. Demographic studies reveal that "American Christians—like the US population as a whole—are becoming more racially and ethnically diverse."[2] The faces representing Christianity are increasingly multicultural with growth among Hispanics and historical black Protestant denominations.[3] This is a challenge in our churches since our social groups generally include those from similar racial and ethnic backgrounds.[4] Recent reports claim that for white Americans, 91 percent of people in their social network are also white. Likeness in black social networks is 84 percent, and 64 percent among Hispanics. Findings also indicate that 75 percent of white Americans report having no friends who are not white. This is clearly in contrast with our future hope where every tribe and nation stand together worshiping God.

In addition, the center of Christianity is shifting.[5] A century ago Europe was home to two-thirds of the world's Christians. Today, no continent can claim to be Christianity's center, because of Christianity's worldwide growth. That said, the dramatic steady growth of Christians in Africa and Asia is opening our eyes to the Global South. As the numbers of white Christians in America declines, there are other voices sitting at the Christian table. We need to listen. Reciprocation involves motion, and difference becomes the Spirit's opportunity. A reciprocal church trusts that the push-and-pull motion among people is to our advantage as the Spirit's multiplying effect is what makes us Christ's church.

Embracing four reciprocal values and practices in your church or ministry will help you join this movement. Yes, these apply to young people in particular. Each of these can also help churches lean into our shared identity as God's people and prioritize God's vital purpose for relationships among all Christians.

1. *Memory.* Communities who celebrate the stories of God's faithfulness will provide young people with a tether in the present and a floodlight for the future. As God's people, these stories tell us who we are and where we come from. We can practice remembering and empower young people to be actors in God's unfolding drama.

2. *Mutuality.* We are in this together. Valuing mutuality is embracing our interdependence and giving special attention to differences, which are quite likely to become opportunities for the Spirit's transforming power. We can practice giving and receiving faith when we empower young people to own faith— not alone but with others. We share the responsibility for one another's faith so all benefit from having one another around.

3. *Contribution.* God created young people to contribute to God's redemptive purposes among us. Christ frees them *from* sin so that they are free *for* God. Valuing contribution first involves seeing this potential in young people. We can practice seeing by identifying their unique gifts and providing space to try these on by contributing to your church's or ministry's mission.

4. *Maturity.* Our rough-edged relationships are designed for receiving the Spirit's power to grow as persons and communities. The Spirit produces community-nurturing fruit that helps us take steps toward reconciliation. We can practice curiosity, and the Spirit generates patience. Fasting temporarily from our personal freedom makes way for the Spirit to generate self-control. When we practice forgiveness, the Spirit generates love. Like windmills along the skyline, transforming relationships act as authentic signs of God's reconciling love.

PLAYING WOOLY BULLY

Have you been to a fifth-grade band concert? Let's be honest, there's a reason tickets aren't sold on StubHub. Listening to songs played by fifty kids who are simultaneously learning to read music and play an instrument is undeniably an act of love. As I look around the room, it fills with a predictable crowd: tired parents, faithful grandparents, brothers and sisters too young to be left home alone, and, of course, the principal. I suspect many of the families represented in this room share our story. Every kid loves getting the new shiny instrument and plays it endlessly—the first week. Then the practice regime begins. Our son plays percussion. Even with the array of noise-making pieces from a drum pad to the triangle to chimes, practicing immediately became a battle in our house. We bribe, he squawks, we plead, he cries, we threaten, he protests. And what's the reward? Spending an hour at a *free* fifth-grade band concert.

The conductor sports a slightly oversized suit and raises his baton signaling to the squirming musicians to stop waving excitedly at their families. The song on the program is "Wooly Bully," a 1965 rock 'n' roll hit by Sam the Sham and the Pharaohs—a classic in American pop culture. My expectations are met by the second measure. We hear a pronounced squeak from a clarinet followed by an out of tune trombone played by a kid whose cheeks resemble a puffer fish. The conductor's baton makes exaggerated motions trying to keep everyone, especially the percussionists, on beat. Trumpets are blasting, sheet music is falling, flutists are awkwardly tilting their heads, and a small girl in the back row is balancing a disproportionately sized tuba compared to the size of her body. A cacophonous sound fills the room.

Suddenly we hear it. At least I think we do. Is it? Yes, we hear it. It's undeniable. The familiar chorus of "Wooly Bully" reverberates in our ears. It goes as quickly as it comes, but nonetheless two parents displaying the scars it took to arrive at this moment now have tears running down their faces. Overwhelmed with pride—the kind only a parent can feel—we hold onto the arm rests to keep from standing up and shouting, "Do you hear it? They are playing 'Wooly Bully'!"

Might this be how our heavenly parent feels when we, the church, for just a moment, figure out how to play a melodious sound together? Isn't this especially true if our heavenly parent was with us during the difficult journey it took to get here? Bearing the scars necessary to overcome our dividing walls and differing wills, Christ rejoices over his people. The Spirit testifies to the glory of God when—even just for a moment—we put our gifts together and produce a sound that serves as an authentic sign of God's redeeming love among us. Yes, sometimes it's gone as quickly as it arrives, but the sound is so sweet, it's undeniable to all who hear.

I now regularly enjoy high school band concerts. Guess what? With lots of practice, that fifth-grade band got better. So can we.

ACKNOWLEDGMENTS

A **RECIPROCAL CHURCH TRUSTS** that the push and pull motion among people is to our advantage as the Spirit's multiplying effect makes us Christ's church. This book exists because of the reciprocating motion of so many.

The seeds for this project were planted during a decade of ministry with outstanding young people in Knoxville, Tennessee. Thank you to my colleagues and friends at Second Presbyterian for your faithful partnership in ministry and treasured memories.

I am grateful for my doctoral studies at Boston College under the direction of Thomas H. Groome and Jane E. Regan. You graciously allowed me to swim in a different Christian pond and opened my eyes to the church. This experience was critical to this project, cemented my research agenda for the coming years, and deeply enriched my own faith. My time at Boston College exemplifies how encounters with "difference" are an opportunity for the Spirit's transforming power. Thank you also to Boston College's Belle Liang for introducing me to your research and inviting me to listen to the experiences of young people. I offer thanks to Andy Root, Luther Seminary, for walking me through the publication process.

I have the privilege of working with colleagues at Gordon College who are also dear friends. Thank you to each member of my department for your genuine interest and refining response to this project. Many thanks to Roger Green for graciously guiding me through my early academic work and mentoring me as a scholar, to Bob Whittet for reminding me that good theology matters when it hits the ground in lived faith, to Mark Cannister for opening up many opportunities and discussing the ideas that fill these pages (plus full credit for suggesting *reciprocal*). Thank you to my teaching assistants who helped with research and revisions at various stages: James Mercier, Eliza Stiles, and Hailey Hill. To all my students in Christian Formation class whose responses sharpened the values and practices in this book. Thank you to my Wednesday faculty prayer group who prayed through this project's rough and celebratory seasons.

I am appreciative of many people at InterVarsity Press: Andrew Bronson, who saw the possibility of this project and offered advice to a new author; Helen Lee, whose wise guidance was crucial in the early stages; thank you to David Fassett and his extraordinary cover design that inspired my definition of reciprocal; and Anna Moseley Gissing, whose careful read and constructive comments enriched this manuscript, and whose belief in this project's value was empowering.

I am forever grateful for my family and the way we journey through life together. Thank you to my brother, John, for cheering me on and providing hotel writing days; to my dad, for long conversations that clarified my thoughts and his good efforts to keep me on a schedule; to my sister, Patty, "my devoted first editor" who read and reread every draft. Nothing I wrote missed her keen eye, insightful comments, and joyful responses. Annie and Mason, thank you for letting me tell our stories, which daily offer me endless insight, and for being proud of your mom. And to Geoff, my love, thank you for gently urging me on with your steady presence.

To the glory of our Creator-Redeemer and prayers for us to embrace the reciprocating motion among us.

DISCUSSION QUESTIONS

CHAPTER 1: EATING MELON ON TUESDAYS

1. How have you reacted to the headlines regarding the loss of young people from the church? In what ways have people in your community responded?

2. What names of young people, and people of all ages, fill your collages? Based on your experience, why did some people continue to embrace the Christian faith while others did not?

3. We are working hard to provide solutions. Which of the four models (the physician, the archaeologist, the engineer, and the coach) might your community be embracing as the solution?

4. Religions need to specialize in the "spiritual" to survive in complex societies, and community is voluntary. Have you seen these play out in your church or ministry?

5. Commodification can be hard to see and maybe even more difficult to admit. How do you hold in tension the truths that God is personal and encounters individuals with the warning that we might commodify or overpersonalize the Christian faith?

6. The gospel package is a minimal version of the Christian message focusing on me and Jesus. What do you think is missing from this gospel?

CHAPTER 2: GALLOPING MARES

1. How do you define the relationship between a person and the church? Compare what you believe to what you see playing out in your church or ministry.

2. In your experience, what draws people to conceive the relationship between a person and the church as either superfluous or supportive?

3. What words or phrases are used in your community to describe sharing the faith with rising generations? How do these words or phrases function (take on unintended meaning) in your community?

4. Examine the roles of adults and young people in your church or ministry. Where are the passer-receiver roles at play? Where does your community resist these prescribed roles?

CHAPTER 3: A VITAL IDENTITY

1. What hesitations do you have about the assertion that churches need to give greater attention to the community?

2. What implications arise from seeing the church as a service provider whose only role is to support a person's relationship with Jesus?

3. Christians are a people belonging to God and have a shared identity. How does this confirm or reshape your view of Christianity?

4. How do young people experience being held in fellowship by Christ in your community, and how might you build on these experiences?

5. What are you coming to understand about the difference between the body of Christ defined as *who we are* (being) and not *what we have* (possession)?

CHAPTER 4: A VITAL PURPOSE

1. In what ways is your church or ministry presently seeking to answer this question: *What is God's intention for the relationship among Christ-followers?*

2. The "ultimate state" is our hope. What about this description stands out to you?

3. Among the three illustrations used to describe the sinful state (Ebenezer Scrooge, Ralph, and Dante), which one resonates with the consequences of sin based on your experience?

4. The reciprocal community asks those who are with-each-other to transform into a people who are for-each-other. What would this look like in your church or ministry?

CHAPTER 5: A VITAL AVENUE

1. How are people taught to make progress toward Christian maturity in your church or ministry? Is maturity more often a solo or a community venture?

2. Read Colossians 3:1-17 twice. Use the singular *you* lens first, and then use the plural *you* lens. How does the meaning of the passage change with each reading?

3. Pick two of the virtues listed in Colossians 3:1-17. How do you imagine these becoming an avenue for the Spirit's work in your community?

4. God dwells with God's people. How does the "temple of the Holy Spirit" metaphor explain this statement as it relates to the church (rather than individuals)?

5. Describe a time when you saw the Spirit's liberating power transform a relationship.

CHAPTER 6: TETHERBALLS AND FLOODLIGHTS

1. What are you coming to understand about God's memory?

2. How might your church be vulnerable to ignoring the past?

3. In your community, are there specific situations that reveal ways in which young people are untethered?

4. What biblical stories act as a tether in your memory?

5. How might valuing memory support a young person's healthy development?

6. How does your church or ministry already practice remembering? Make a list of your church's "remember when" events. Think about both the biblical narrative as well as your community's specific story. What other "remember when" moments might you add to this list?

CHAPTER 7: THE OXPECKER'S GIFT

1. In what ways do we (and do we not) treat young people as indispensable to our churches and ministries (1 Corinthians 12)?

2. What hesitations do you have about the claim "differences are an opportunity"? What about this claim gives you hope?

3. Have you observed the one-way relationship flow between adults and young people in your church or ministry? What did it look like?

4. Which of the relational processes (authenticity, empathy, collaboration, and companionship) are already at work in adult-youth relationships in your community? Which one might be missing? Ask a young person the same question and compare answers.

5. We are in this together. In what ways does your church or ministry benefit from having young people around?

CHAPTER 8: SEEING BEYOND THE EPIDEMIC

1. What fears do you think drive the epidemic narrative in your community? Do you see the *fixing* posture among adults (parents, pastors, leaders, etc.)? What deficits do people perceive in young people that need to be overcome?

2. Do certain young people come to mind as you read about the problem and potential lenses? How does your response to them change when each lens is in use?

3. Evaluate your programs, teaching, and recent decisions. Both the problem and potential lenses are likely present, but does one persist over the other?

4. What are you coming to understand about *seeing potential* based on the description of God as Creator-Redeemer?

5. Imagine young people hearing us emphasize the *for* in addition to the *from* (Christ saves us *from* our sins to free us *for* God.) How might this change affect what you choose to teach, prioritize, and fund?

CHAPTER 9: MOVING BEYOND THE EPIDEMIC

1. In what ways is your church or ministry already seeing potential in young people? How might you build on this?

2. Give an example of young people *participating* in what your church or ministry is already doing. Can you also give an example of a young person contributing by enriching or maybe even changing what you do?

3. What would it look like in your community to share power with young people?

4. What hesitations do you have about being a space maker for young people to practice using their gifts? Are there ways you can imagine space-making being a success?

5. Consider showing your church's mission statement to a group of young people, and asking them how they might help the church carry out its mission.

CHAPTER 10: WINDMILLS OF HOPE

1. Which of the following labels is most concerning to you? Do any of these describe you?

> *the dones*—those who are simply done with Christianity

> *the nones*—those who check the box "none" when asked their religious affiliation

> *the spiritual but not religious*—those who welcome the divine but reject religious institutions

2. Paul names specific relationships needing liberation in Galatians 3:28: the ethnic separation amid Jews and Greeks, the economic and social separation between slave and free, and the gender divisions among males and females. In your community, what might characterize the liberation needed among young people and adults?

3. Which of the practices do you find most challenging: curiosity, fasting, or forgiveness? What effects have you seen on relationships when you did (and didn't) carry out these practices?

4. What would need to change (budgets, priorities, commitment, etc.) in your church or ministry for relationship windmills to more readily fill the skylines of our cities and towns? Why?

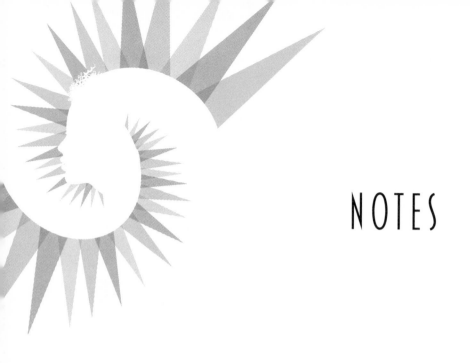

NOTES

INTRODUCTION: RECIPROCAL CHURCH

[1]Dorothy C. Bass, ed., *Practicing Our Faith: A Way of Life for a Searching People*, 2nd ed. (San Francisco: Jossey-Bass, 2010); Adele Ahlberg Calhoun, *Spiritual Disciplines Handbook: Practices That Transform Us*, rev. and exp. ed. (Downers Grove, IL: InterVarsity Press, 2015); James K. A. Smith, *You Are What You Love: The Spiritual Power of Habit* (Grand Rapids: Brazos, 2016); and Mike King, *Presence-Centered Youth Ministry: Guiding Students into Spiritual Formation* (Downers Grove, IL: InterVarsity Press, 2006).

[2]Patrick M. Lencioni, "Make Your Values Mean Something," *Harvard Business Review*, July 1, 2002, https://hbr.org/2002/07/make-your-values -mean-something.

1 EATING MELON ON TUESDAYS

[1]Christian Smith and Melinda Denton Lundquist, *Soul Searching: The Religious and Spiritual Lives of American Teenagers* (Oxford: Oxford University Press, 2005); Christian Smith and Patricia Snell, *Souls in Transition: The Religious and Spiritual Lives of Emerging Adults* (New York: Oxford University Press, 2009); Kenda Creasy Dean, *Almost Christian: What the Faith of Our Teenagers Is Telling the American Church* (New York: Oxford

University Press, 2010); Christian Smith et al., *Lost in Transition: The Dark Side of Emerging Adulthood* (Oxford: Oxford University Press, 2011); "Most Twentysomethings Put Christianity on the Shelf Following Spiritually Active Teen Years," Barna.com, September 11, 2006, www.barna.com /research/most-twentysomethings-put-christianity-on-the-shelf-following -spiritually-active-teen-years; David Kinnaman and Aly Hawkins, *You Lost Me: Why Young Christians Are Leaving Church and Rethinking Faith* (Grand Rapids: Baker, 2011); "America's Changing Religious Landscape," Pew Research Center, May 12, 2015, www.pewforum.org/2015/05/12 /americas-changing-religious-landscape; Frank Newport, "Percentage of Christians in U.S. Drifting Down, but Still High," *Gallup.com*, December 24, 2015, http://news.gallup.com/poll/187955/percentage-christians -drifting-down-high.aspx; "Atheism Doubles Among Generation Z," Barna.com, January 24, 2018, www.barna.com/research/atheism-doubles -among-generation-z.

[2]Andy Root presses this point further by declaring that practical theology has uncritically adopted the social sciences without prioritizing theological interests. Andrew Root, *Christopraxis: A Practical Theology of the Cross* (Minneapolis: Fortress, 2014).

[3]Joshua Packard, "Meet the 'Dones,'" *CT Pastors*, accessed March 10, 2018, www.christianitytoday.com/pastors/2015/summer-2015/meet-dones.html; Michael Lipka, "Why America's 'Nones' Left Religion Behind," Pew Research Center, August 24, 2016, www.pewresearch.org/fact-tank/2016/08/24 /why-americas-nones-left-religion-behind; Barna Research, "Meet Those Who 'Love Jesus but Not the Church,'" Barna.com, March 30, 2017, www .barna.com/research/meet-love-jesus-not-church.

[4]Andrew Root and Kenda Creasy Dean, *The Theological Turn in Youth Ministry* (Downers Grove, IL: InterVarsity Press, 2011), 16.

[5]David F. White, *Practicing Discernment with Youth: A Transformative Youth Ministry Approach* (Cleveland: Pilgrim Press, 2005); Katherine Turpin, *Branded: Adolescents Converting from Consumer Faith* (Cleveland: Pilgrim Press, 2006); Kenda Creasy Dean, *Practicing Passion: Youth and the Quest for a Passionate Church* (Grand Rapids: Eerdmans, 2004); and Andrew Root, *Revisiting Relational Youth Ministry: From a Strategy of Influence to a Theology of Incarnation* (Downers Grove, IL: InterVarsity Press, 2007).

[6]For a helpful overview of ecclesiology from a historical perspective, see Veli-Matti Kärkkäinen, *An Introduction to Ecclesiology: Ecumenical, Historical & Global Perspectives* (Downers Grove, IL: IVP Academic, 2002).

[7]R. D. Putnam, *Bowling Alone: The Collapse and Revival of American Community* (New York: Simon & Schuster, 2000).

[8]Robert Wuthnow, "Small Groups Forge New Notions of Community and the Sacred," *Christian Century*, December 8, 1993, 1236-40.

[9]I am using Johannes Först's outline of Luhmann's theory and subsequent implications for the church. Johannes Först, "Functional Secularization and Conversion: On the Changed Demands Made on Ministerial Action in the Catholic Church," in *Rabbi, Pastor, Priest: Their Roles and Profiles Through the Ages*, ed. Walter Homolka and Heinz-Günther Schöttler (Berlin: Walter de Gruyter, 2013), 245-57.

[10]Many others argue this point, for example, Tom Beaudoin, *Consuming Faith: Integrating Who We Are with What We Buy* (Lanham, MD: Rowman & Littlefield, 2003); and Smith et al., *Lost in Transition*.

[11]V. J. Miller, *Consuming Religion: Christian Faith and Practice in a Consumer Culture* (New York: Continuum International, 2005), 30.

[12]Thanks to my friend and colleague Teri Elliot-Hart for clarifying the pervasive role of commodification in advertising.

[13]Turpin, *Branded*, 54-55.

[14]Drive Thru Church, "NewSong Edit," Newsonmedia, 2007, https://www.youtube.com/watch?v=b7sR2CxptJE.

[15]Sharon Galgay Ketcham, "Solving the Retention Problem Through Integration: A Communal Vision for Youth Ministry," *Journal of Youth Ministry* 11, no. 1 (2012): 7-29.

2 GALLOPING MARES

[1]Dietrich Bonhoeffer, *Life Together and Prayerbook of the Bible*, Dietrich Bonhoeffer Works 5 (Minneapolis: Augsburg Fortress Press, 2005), 34-38.

[2]Robert Fuller, *Spiritual, but Not Religious: Understanding Unchurched America* (Oxford: Oxford University Press, 2001).

[3]Smith and Lundquist, *Soul Searching*, 251-52; and Smith and Snell, *Souls in Transition*, 113.

[4]Jefferson Bethke, "Why I Hate Religion, but Love Jesus," YouTube, January 10, 2012, www.youtube.com/watch?v=1IAhDGYlpqY.

[5]David Augsburger, *Dissident Discipleship* (Grand Rapids: Brazos, 2006), 7-22. Anabaptists include the Mennonites, Amish, and Brethren churches. For Augsburger the answer to both of these questions is a resounding no. Instead, he is promoting a distinct vision of the Christian life that claims other people as integral to a maturing Christian faith.

[6]Augustine, *Confessions*, ed. Michael P. Foley, trans. F. J. Sheed, 2nd ed. (Indianapolis: Hackett, 2006), 3.

[7]Augsburger, *Dissident Discipleship*, 14.

[8]Darlene Zschech, "I Give You My Heart," *God Is in the House,* Hillsong Music Australia, 1996.

[9]I have written on this in greater detail in: Sharon Galgay Ketcham, "Solving the Retention Problem through Integration: A Communal Vision for Youth Ministry," *Journal of Youth Ministry* 11, no. 1 (2012): 7-29.

[10]J. White, *Holy Wow: Boost Your Youth Ministry Creativity* (Loveland: Group, 2004), 12.

[11]M. P. Strommen and R. A. Hardel, *Passing On the Faith: A Radical New Model for Youth and Family Ministry* (Winona, MN: St. Mary's Press, 2000).

[12]Kenda Creasy and Foster Dean Ron, *The Godbearing Life: The Art of Soul Tending for Youth Ministry* (Nashville: Upper Room Books, 1998), 99 (italics added).

[13]Ketcham, "Solving the Retention Problem through Integration."

3 A VITAL IDENTITY

[1]For historical accounts of youth ministry in America, see Mark Senter, *The Coming Revolution in Youth Ministry and Its Radical Impact on the Church* (Wheaton, IL: Scripture Press, 1992); Mark Senter, *When God Shows Up: A History of Protestant Youth Ministry in America* (Grand Rapids: Baker Academic, 2010); Mark Cannister, "Youth Ministry Pioneers of the 20th Century: Part 1, Frederick and Arthur Wood, Lloyd Bryant, Percy Crawford, and Evelyn McClusky," *Christian Education Journal* 3, no. 1 (2003): 66-72; and Thomas E. Bergler, *The Juvenilization of American Christianity* (Grand Rapids: Eerdmans, 2012).

[2]Peter T. O'Brien, *Colossians, Philemon*, Word Biblical Commentary 44 (Waco, TX: Word, 1982), 160-165.

[3]Chap Clark, ed., *Adoptive Youth Ministry: Integrating Emerging Generations into the Family of Faith* (Grand Rapids: Baker Academic, 2016).

[4]Stanley J. Grenz, *Theology for the Community of God* (Nashville: Broadman & Holman, 1994); and Jennifer Eyl, "Semantic Voids, New Testament Translation, and Anachronism: The Case of Paul's Use of Ekklēsia," *Method and Theory in the Study of Religion* 26, nos. 4-5 (2014): 322.

[5]Dianne Bergant, "Memorial, Memory," in *New Interpreter's Dictionary of the Bible*, ed. Katharine Doob Sakenfeld (Nashville: Abingdon Press, 2009), 4:644.

[6]Ellen T. Charry, "Sacramental Ecclesiology," in *The Community of the Word: Toward an Evangelical Ecclesiology*, ed. Mark Husbands and Daniel J. Treier (Downers Grove, IL: IVP Academic, 2005), 205 (italics added).

[7]Charry, "Sacramental Ecclesiology," 205.

[8]There is a lively debate among scholars on whether the Septuagint or the Greco-Roman world was of greater influence on the New Testament author's choice of *ekklesia*. Regardless of position, identity is central to its use. See Paul Trebilco, "The Significance of the Distribution of Self-Designations in Acts," *Novum Testamentum* 54, no. 1 (2012): 30-49; G. K. Beale, "The Background of Ἐκκλησία Revisited," *Journal for the Study of the New Testament* 38, no. 2 (December 2015): 151-68.

[9]Walter Brueggemann, "The Book of Exodus," in *The New Interpreter's Bible* (Nashville: Abingdon Press, 1994), 1:839.

[10]Eyl, "Semantic Voids"; Beale, "Background of Ἐκκλησία Revisited"; Trebilco, "Significance of the Distribution of Self-Designations in Acts."

[11]Stephen James Walton, "Calling the Church Names: Learning About Christian Identity from Acts," *Perspectives in Religious Studies* 41, no. 3 (September 2014): 241.

[12]For example, John Calvin emphasizes the invisible church, described as all genuine believers united through the Holy Spirit.

[13]Emil Brunner, *The Misunderstanding of the Church*, trans. Harold Knight (Philadelphia: Westminster Press, 1952), 9-10.

[14]Brunner, *Misunderstanding of the Church*, 10-11.

[15]Bonhoeffer, *Life Together*, 5:32.

[16]Luke Timothy Johnson, "The Body in Question: The Social Complexities of Resurrection," in *Unity and Diversity in the Gospels and Paul: Essays in Honor of Frank J. Matera*, ed. Christopher W. Skinner and Kelly R. Iverson (Atlanta: Society of Biblical Literature, 2012), 225-28.

[17]Johnson, "Body in Question," 229.

4 A VITAL PURPOSE

[1]Clifford J. Green, *Bonhoeffer: A Theology of Sociality* (Grand Rapids: Eerdmans, 1999), 47.

[2]Dietrich Bonhoeffer, *Sanctorum Communio: A Theological Study of the Sociology of the Church*, Dietrich Bonhoeffer Works 1 (Minneapolis: Fortress Press, 1998), 63.

[3]Bonhoeffer, *Sanctorum Communio*, 83.

[4]Miroslav Volf, "Love Your Heavenly Enemy: How Are We Going to Live Eternally with Those We Can't Stand Now?" *Christianity Today* 44, no. 12 (2000): 94-97.

[5]Volf, "Love Your Heavenly Enemy," 96.

[6]Volf, "Love Your Heavenly Enemy," 97.

[7]Bonhoeffer, *Sanctorum Communio*, 107.

[8]Bonhoeffer, *Sanctorum Communio*, 145.

[9]Charles Dickens, *A Christmas Carol* (n.p.: Plain Label Books, 2010), 169.

[10]William Golding, *Lord of the Flies* (New York: Penguin, 1959), 185.

[11]Dante Alighieri, *The Divine Comedy*, trans. Carlyle-Wicksteed (New York: Modern Library, 1932), 29.

[12]Alighieri, *Divine Comedy*, 175.

[13]Bonhoeffer, *Sanctorum Communio*, 108.

[14]Bonhoeffer, *Sanctorum Communio*, 120.

[15]Bonhoeffer, *Sanctorum Communio*, 173.

5 A VITAL AVENUE

[1]"Meaning inevitably derives from the general social system of the speakers of a language." Bruce Malina, *The New Testament World: Insights from Cultural Anthropology*, 3rd ed. (Louisville: Westminster John Knox Press, 2001), 1.

[2]Malina, *New Testament World*, 27-41.

[3]Peter T. O'Brien, *Colossians, Philemon*, Word Biblical Commentary 44 (Waco, TX: Word, 1982), xxxi-6. Much scholarly work focused on naming the "Colossian heresy." Recently scholars are less concerned with putting forward a new heresy; rather, they argue for the most probable among the heresies.

[4]O'Brien, *Colossians, Philemon*, 160.

[5]Ben Witherington III, *The Letters to Philemon, the Colossians, and the Ephesians: A Socio-Rhetorical Commentary on the Captivity Epistles* (Grand Rapids: Eerdmans, 2007), 176.

[6]Walter Brueggemann, "The Book of Exodus," in *The New Interpreter's Bible* (Nashville: Abingdon Press, 1994), 1:678-79.

[7]Irenaeus, "St. Irenaeus of Lyons Against the Heresies," trans. and annotated Dominic J. Unger and John J. Dillon, Ancient Christian Writers 55 (New York: Paulist Press, 1992), 3.24.1.

[8]Pannenberg uses the word *ecstatic* to emphasize the Spirit's power acting in ways that are beyond human ability. Wolfhart Pannenberg, *Systematic Theology* (Grand Rapids: Eerdmans, 1991), 3:133.

[9]David S. Dockery, "An Outline of Paul's View of the Spiritual Life: Foundation for an Evangelical Spirituality," *Criswell Theological Review* 3 (1989): 329.

[10]Veli-Matti Kärkkäinen, *An Introduction to Ecclesiology: Ecumenical, Historical & Global Perspectives* (Downers Grove, IL: IVP Academic, 2002), 231.

6 TETHERBALLS AND FLOODLIGHTS

[1]Stanley J. Grenz, *Theology for the Community of God* (Nashville: Broadman & Holman, 1994), 89-91.

[2]Dianne Bergant, "Memorial, Memory," in *New Interpreter's Dictionary of the Bible*, ed. Katharine Doob Sakenfeld (Nashville: Abingdon Press, 2009), 4:31.

[3]Allen Verhey, "Remember, Remembrance," ed. David Noel Freedman, *Anchor Bible Dictionary* 5 (New York: Anchor Books, 1992): 667-69.

[4]Ronald S. Hendel, "Remember," in *New Interpreter's Dictionary of the Bible Volume*, ed. Katharine Doob Sakenfeld (Nashville: Abingdon Press, 2009), 4:761.

[5]Hendel, "Remember," 761.

[6]D. L. Mayfield, "Facing Our Legacy of Lynching," *Christianity Today*, August 18, 2017, www.christianitytoday.com/ct/2017/september/legacy-lynching-america-christians-repentance.html.

[7]Mark DeYmaz and George Yancey, *Building a Healthy Multi-Ethnic Church: Mandate, Commitments and Practices of a Diverse Congregation* (San Francisco: Jossey-Bass, 2007); Brenda Salter McNeil and Tony Campolo, *A Credible Witness: Reflections on Power, Evangelism and Race* (Downers

Grove, IL: InterVarsity Press, 2008); Daniel Hill, *White Awake: An Honest Look at What It Means to Be White* (Downers Grove: InterVarsity Press, 2017); Michael O. Emerson and Christian Smith, *Divided by Faith: Evangelical Religion and the Problem of Race in America* (Oxford: Oxford University Press, 2001).

[8]David Elkind, *All Grown Up and No Place to Go: Teenagers in Crisis*, rev. ed. (Reading, Mass: Da Capo Press, 1998), 190.

[9]"Study Finds Depression on Rise in Adolescents but Particularly Among Teen Girls," American Academy of Pediatrics, November 14, 2016, www.aap .org/en-us/about-the-aap/aap-press-room/pages/Study-Finds-Depression -On-Rise-In-Adolescents-But-Particularly-Among-Teen-Girls.aspx.

[10]Belle Liang et al., "The Mediating Role of Engagement in Mentoring Relationships and Self-Esteem Among Affluent Adolescent Girls," *Psychology in the Schools* 53, no. 8 (September 2016): 848-60.

[11]Susanna Schrobsdorff, "Teen Depression and Anxiety: Why the Kids Are Not Alright," *Time*, October 26, 2016, http://time.com/4547322/american -teens-anxious-depressed-overwhelmed.

[12]Jean M. Twenge, *iGen: Why Today's Super-Connected Kids Are Growing up Less Rebellious, More Tolerant, Less Happy—and Completely Unprepared for Adulthood—and What That Means for the Rest of Us* (New York City: Atria Books, 2017).

[13]Jean M. Twenge, "Have Smartphones Destroyed a Generation?" *The Atlantic*, September 2017, www.theatlantic.com/magazine/archive/2017/09/has-the -smartphone-destroyed-a-generation/534198/?utm_source=nl-atlantic -weekly-080417.

[14]Barry Schwartz, "More Isn't Always Better," *Harvard Business Review*, June 2006, https://hbr.org/2006/06/more-isnt-always-better.

[15]W. Andrews Collins and Laurence Steinberg, "Adolescent Development in Interpersonal Context," in *Handbook of Child Psychology: Theoretical Models of Human Development*, ed. William Damon and Richard M. Lerner, 6th ed. (Hoboken, NJ: John Wiley, 2006), 1:1003-67.

[16]Collins and Steinberg base this claim on research conducted by Roy Baumeister and Dianne M. Tice. See R. Baumeister and D. Tice, "How Adolescence Became the Struggle for Self: A Historical Transformation of

Psychological Development," in *Psychological Perspectives on Self*, ed. J. Suls and A. Greenewald (Hillsdale, NJ: Erlbaum, 1986), 3:183-201.

[17]Collins and Steinberg, "Adolescent Development in Interpersonal Context," 1034.

[18]Wright's fifth act analogy is part of a larger discussion on the authority of the Bible. He is addressing an interpretation of authority as "fixed" and "absolute," especially among evangelicals, and proposes an alternative view of how God exercises authority through the biblical story that includes human engagement with the story itself. N. T. Wright, "How Can the Bible Be Authoritative?" *Vox Evangelica*, December 10, 2013, 1-20.

[19]Anna Moseley Gissing and Cate MacDonald, *Let Us Keep the Feast: Living the Church Year at Home*, ed. Jessica Snell (Oro Valley, AZ: Doulos Resources, 2013).

[20]Christy Nockels, Daniel Carson, Jesse Reeves, Kristian Stanfill, and Matthew Maher, "Lord, I Need You," *Lord, I Need You*, Provident Label Group, accessed August 8, 2017, www.worshiptogether.com/songs/lord-i-need-you.

[21]"Heidelberg Catechism," in *The Book of Confessions* (Louisville, KY: Westminster/John Knox Press, 1999).

7 THE OXPECKER'S GIFT

[1]James M. Howard, *Paul, the Community, and Progressive Sanctification: An Exploration into Community-Based Transformation Within Pauline Theology*, Studies in Biblical Literature 90 (New York: Peter Lang, 2007), 108.

[2]Kenda Creasy Dean, *Practicing Passion: Youth and the Quest for a Passionate Church* (Grand Rapids: Eerdmans, 2004).

[3]Ruth M. Bancewicz, "What Animals Teach Christians About Getting Along," *Christianity Today*, March 24, 2017, www.christianitytoday.com/ct/2017/march-web-only/what-animals-teach-christians-about-getting-along.html.

[4]Urie Bronfenbrenner and Pamela A. Morris, "The Ecology of Developmental Processes," in *Handbook of Child Psychology*, ed. William Damon and Richard M. Lerner, 5th ed. (New York: John Wiley, 1998), 1:996. Pioneers in the field of positive youth development (PYD) such as William Damon, Richard Learner, and Peter Benson have built on Bronfenbrenner's theory over the last two decades and reshaped how we research and think about adolescent development.

[5]Richard M. Lerner, *Concepts and Theories of Human Development*, 3rd ed. (Mahwah, NJ: Lawrence Erlbaum, 2002), 16-20.; Urie Bronfenbrenner, ed., *Making Humans Beings Human: Bioecological Perspectives on Human Development* (Thousand Oaks, CA: Sage, 2005); and Bronfenbrenner and Morris, "Ecology of Developmental Processes."

[6]Bronfenbrenner and Morris, "Ecology of Developmental Processes," 997.

[7]Bronfenbrenner and Morris, "Ecology of Developmental Processes," 997.

[8]Richard M. Lerner, "Relative Plasticity, Integration, Temporality, and Diversity in Human Development: A Developmental Contextual Perspective About Theory, Process, and Method," *Developmental Psychology* 32, no. 4 (1996): 782.

[9]Renee Spencer, "Understanding the Mentoring Process Between Adolescents and Adults," *Youth and Society* 37, no. 3 (March 2006): 289.

[10]John H. Westerhoff, *Will Our Children Have Faith?* (Minneapolis: Seabury Press, 1976), 17.

[11]Miroslav Volf, *After Our Likeness: The Church as the Image of the Trinity* (Grand Rapids: Eerdmans, 1998).

[12]Volf, *After Our Likeness*, 149.

[13]Volf, *After Our Likeness*, 150.

[14]This statement is part of Volf's construction of a free-church ecclesiology. For Volf, this is how the church comes into existence based on Matthew 18:20. Calling on the name of Christ is confession, and when this is done with others who make the same confession, we are promised Christ's presence. Christ's presence constitutes and sustains the church. Volf, *After Our Likeness*.

[15]Westerhoff, *Will Our Children Have Faith?* 33.

[16]Howard, *Paul, the Community, and Progressive Sanctification*, 97.

8 SEEING BEYOND THE EPIDEMIC

[1]Chris Elliott, "The Reader's Editor On . . . Negative Portrayals of Teenagers in the Media," *Guardian*, July 7, 2013, www.theguardian.com/comment isfree/2013/jul/07/open-door-negative-portrayals-teenagers-media.

[2]Alison Gopnik, "What's Wrong With the Teenage Mind?" *Wall Street Journal*, January 28, 2012, www.wsj.com/articles/SB1000142405297020380 6504577181351486558984.

[3]G. Stanley Hall, quoted in Richard M. Lerner, "Promoting Positive Youth Development: Theoretical and Empirical Bases" (workshop, National Research Council, Washington, DC, September 9, 2005), 4.

[4]William Damon, "What Is Positive Youth Development?" *Annals of the American Academy of Political and Social Science* 591 (2004): 14.

[5]Erik H. Erikson, *Childhood and Society*, 2nd ed. (New York: Norton, 1963); and Erik H. Erikson, *Identity, Youth and Crisis* (New York: Norton, 1968).

[6]Lerner, "Promoting Positive Youth Development," 5.

[7]Lerner, "Promoting Positive Youth Development," 5.

[8]Damon, "What Is Positive Youth Development?" 14.

[9]"What Happens When We Notice the Good Stuff?" Search Institute, December 2, 2015, http://hosted.verticalresponse.com/833119/a95f1cbfd3/1544 006475/6f1dfe2e9f.

[10]Damon, "What Is Positive Youth Development?" 15.

[11]Peter L. Benson et al., "Positive Youth Development: Theory, Research, and Applications," in *Handbook of Child Psychology: Theoretical Models of Human Development*, ed. William Damon and Richard M. Lerner (Hoboken, NJ: John Wiley, 2006), 1:899.

[12]Peter L. Benson, "Sparks: How Youth Thrive," TEDx Talks, April 2011, www .youtube.com/watch?v=TqzUHcW58Us&feature=related.

[13]"Atheism Doubles Among Generation Z," Barna.com, January 24, 2018, www.barna.com/research/atheism-doubles-among-generation-z.

[14]Paulo Freire and Donaldo Macedo, *Pedagogy of the Oppressed*, trans. Myra Bergman Ramos, 30th anniv. ed. (New York: Bloomsbury Academic, 2000), 72.

[15]Chap Clark, *Hurt: Inside the World of Today's Teenagers* (Grand Rapids: Baker Academic, 2004).

[16]Nel Noddings, *Caring: A Feminine Approach to Ethics and Moral Education*, 2nd ed. (Berkeley: University of California Press, 2003); Nel Noddings, *The Challenge to Care in Schools: An Alternative Approach to Education*, 2nd ed., Advances in Contemporary Educational Thought (New York: Teachers College Press, 2005).

[17]Wendy Mogel, *The Blessing of a Skinned Knee: Using Jewish Teachings to Raise Self-Reliant Children* (New York: Scribner, 2001); and Wendy Mogel, *The Blessing of a B Minus: Using Jewish Teachings to Raise Resilient Teenagers* (New York: Scribner, 2011).

[18]Mogel, *Blessing of a Skinned Knee*, 33.

[19]Justo L. González, *A Concise History of Christian Doctrine* (Nashville: Abingdon Press, 2006), 38-41.

[20]Thomas H. Groome, *Christian Religious Education: Sharing Our Story and Vision* (San Francisco: Harper & Row, 1980), 83-89.

9 MOVING BEYOND THE EPIDEMIC

[1]Marc Cortez, *Theological Anthropology: A Guide for the Perplexed* (New York: Bloomsbury, 2010), 37-40.

[2]For example, see discussion of the *imago Dei* in Stanley J. Grenz, *Theology for the Community of God* (Nashville: Broadman & Holman, 1994); and Daniel L. Migliore, *Faith Seeking Understanding: An Introduction to Christian Theology*, 3rd ed. (Grand Rapids: Eerdmans, 2014).

[3]Cortez, *Theological Anthropology*, 17.

[4]Migliore, *Faith Seeking Understanding*, 128.

[5]Sharon Galgay Ketcham, "Youth," in *Evangelical Dictionary of Theology*, ed. Daniel J. Treier and Walter A. Elwell, 3rd ed. (Grand Rapids: Baker Academic, 2017).

[6]Andrew Root, *Faith Formation in a Secular Age: Responding to the Church's Obsession with Youthfulness* (Grand Rapids: Baker Academic, 2017); and Thomas E. Bergler, "The Juvenilization of American Christianity," (Grand Rapids: Eerdmans, 2012).

[7]Richard M. Lerner, Celia B. Fisher, and Richard Weinberg, "Toward a Science for and of the People: Promoting Civil Society Through the Application of Developmental Science," *Child Development* 71, no. 1 (February 2000): 11-20; and Richard M. Lerner, *Liberty: Thriving and Civic Engagement Among America's Youth* (Thousand Oaks, CA: Sage, 2004).

[8]William Damon, *The Path to Purpose: Helping Our Children Find Their Calling in Life* (New York: Free Press, 2008).

[9]Helen Fox, *Their Highest Vocation: Social Justice and the Millennial Generation* (New York: International Academic Publishers, 2011); and Christian Smith and Patricia Snell, *Souls in Transition: The Religious and Spiritual Lives of Emerging Adults* (New York: Oxford University Press, 2009).

[10]Eugene C. Roehlkepartain et al., *Relationships First: Creating Connections That Help Young People Thrive* (Minneapolis: Search Institute, 2017), 4.

[11]For a helpful theoretical and practical approach to teaching young people to be contributors, see David F. White, *Practicing Discernment with Youth: A Transformative Youth Ministry Approach* (Cleveland: Pilgrim Press, 2005).

[12]Peter C. Scales, Peter L. Benson, and Eugene C. Roehlkepartain, "Adolescent Thriving: The Role of Sparks, Relationships, and Empowerment," *Journal of Youth Adolescence* 40 (2011): 264.

[13]Scales, Benson, and Roehlkepartain, "Adolescent Thriving."

[14]Scales, Benson, and Roehlkepartain, "Adolescent Thriving," 274; Peter Scales, *Other People's Kids: Social Expectations and American Adults' Involvement with Children and Adolescents* (New York: Kluwer Academic/Plenum, 2003).

10 WINDMILLS OF HOPE

[1]Michael Lipka, "Why America's 'Nones' Left Religion Behind," Pew Research Center, August 24, 2016, www.pewresearch.org/fact -tank/2016/08/24/why-americas-nones-left-religion-behind. The research needs to be read carefully in order to best interpret the results based on what questions are asked and what comparisons are being made, as well as what aspects of religiosity are being measured.

[2]Gregory A. Smith and Alan Cooperman, "The Factors Driving the Growth of Religious 'Nones' in the U.S.," Pew Research Center, September 14, 2016, www.pewresearch.org/fact-tank/2016/09/14/the-factors-driving-the -growth-of-religious-nones-in-the-u-s.

[3]"Atheism Doubles Among Generation Z," Barna.com, January 24, 2018, www.barna.com/research/atheism-doubles-among-generation-z.

[4]David Kinnaman and Aly Hawkins, *You Lost Me: Why Young Christians Are Leaving Church and Rethinking Faith* (Grand Rapids: Baker, 2011).

[5]Jeffrey Jensen Arnett, *Emerging Adulthood: The Winding Road from the Late Teens Through the Twenties* (New York: Oxford University Press, 2006), 218-20.

[6]J. J. Arnett and L. A. Jensen, "A Congregation of One: Individualized Religious Beliefs Among Emerging Adults," *Journal of Adolescent Research* 17 (2002): 463.

[7]James Strong, *Strong's Exhaustive Concordance* (Peabody, MA: Hendrickson, 2007), 71.

[8]Mike Yaconelli, *Messy Spirituality* (Grand Rapids: Zondervan, 2007).

[9]J. Paul Sampley, Richard B. Hays, Judith Gundry-Volf, Morna Hooker, and Andrew T. Lincoln, *2 Corinthians-Philemon*, New Interpreter's Bible 11 (Nashville: Abingdon, 2000), 534.

[10]Sampley et al., *2 Corinthians-Philemon*, 183-84.

[11]James M. Howard, *Paul, the Community, and Progressive Sanctification: An Exploration into Community-Based Transformation within Pauline Theology*, Studies in Biblical Literature 90 (New York: Peter Lang, 2007), 141.

[12]J. Louis Martyn, *Galatians: A New Translation with Introduction and Commentary*, Anchor Bible (New York: Doubleday, 1997), 524, n. 49.

[13]Sampley et al., *2 Corinthians-Philemon*, 187.

[14]Martyn, *Galatians*, 484.

[15]Howard, *Paul, the Community, and Progressive Sanctification*, 143.

[16]Brene Brown, *Rising Strong: How the Ability to Reset Transforms the Way We Live, Love, Parent, and Lead* (New York: Random House, 2017), 99-129.

[17]John Chrysostom, *On Repentance and Almsgiving*, Fathers of the Church 96 (Washington, DC: Catholic University of America Press, 2010), 57.

[18]Martin Luther King Jr., *Strength to Love* (Philadelphia: Fortress Press, 1981), 51.

[19]Jacob Jones, Wislene Augustin, and Benjami Suprice, "Practicing Forgiveness" (Christian Formation and Culture, Gordon College, November 2016).

[20]Dietrich Bonhoeffer, *Life Together and Prayerbook of the Bible*, Dietrich Bonhoeffer Works (Minneapolis: Augsburg Fortress Press, 2005), 32-35.

EPILOGUE: FAITH FLOURISHES WITH PRACTICE

[1]Soong-Chan Rah, *Prophetic Lament: A Call for Justice in Troubled Times* (Downers Grove, IL: InterVarsity Press, 2015).

[2]"America's Changing Religious Landscape," Pew Research Center, May 12, 2015, www.pewforum.org/2015/05/12/americas-changing -religious-landscape.

[3]Daniel Cox and Robert P. Jones, "America's Changing Religious Identity," Public Religion Research Institute, September 9, 2017, www.prri.org /research/american-religious-landscape-christian-religiously-unaffiliated.

[4]Daniel Cox, Juhem Navarro-Rivera, and Robert P. Jones, "Race, Religion, and Political Affiliation of Americans' Core Social Networks," PRRI, August

3, 2016, www.prri.org/research/poll-race-religion-politics-americans
-social-networks.

[5]"Global Christianity—A Report on the Size and Distribution of the
World's Christian Population," Pew Research Center, December 19, 2011,
www.pewforum.org/2011/12/19/global-christianity-exec.